ZOHRA SEGAL

'Fatty'

In what has been termed her comeback film, Zohra Segal played the role of Amitabh Bachchan's mother in Cheeni Kum

ZOHRA SEGAL

'Fatty'

Kiran Segal

NIYOGI BOOKS

Published by
NIYOGI BOOKS
D-78, Okhla Industrial Area, Phase-I
New Delhi-110 020, India
Tel: 91-11-26816301, 49327000
Fax: 91-11-26810483, 26813830
email: niyogibooks@gmail.com
www.niyogibooks.com

Design: Write Media

ISBN: 978-93-81523-35-3
Year of Publication: 2012

Printed at: Niyogi Offset Pvt. Ltd., New Delhi, India

CONTENTS

With Preity Zinta in Veer-Zaara, 2004

FOREWORD

When someone asked me to write a book on my mother I wondered, "What can I write about her? She is my mother and that's it." Most important, I am not a writer—far from it. I can only dance and nothing else!

Then the seed was sown and I kept thinking about it as the days went by. This was in 2006, almost six years ago. My mind travelled in reverse gear to my childhood with her, my father Kameshwar Segal and my brother Pavan in 41 Pali Hill, Mumbai

Kiran Segal with her mother in London—together, the two have been through several ups and downs in the journey of life

(then Bombay). What a happy family we were. Her strictness, my father's laughter, the get-togethers with the neighbours, my friends and I running all over the place, going to school and of course going to Prithvi Theatres with her. My first dance lessons and training were with my mother and I learnt a lot from watching her teach 'dance'.

I have written this book not as a historian or an experienced writer but as a daughter who has been with her mother throughout her mother's 'ups' and 'downs', her struggle, her tragedies and her several moods! My mother has also been a great friend to me. We've had our fights, disagreements and criticisms of each other–more her than me–our jokes on ourselves and on others. It has been wonderful.

On 27 April 2012 my mother Zohra Segal completes a hundred years of excitement in dance, theatre, films, television and this journey we call life. She claims, "I have a hundred years of history in me!"

Congratulations, Ammi!

Kiran Segal
7 March 2012

HER ROOTS

She dates her ancestry way back to AD 1361 to a Jew called Quais from Afghanistan. He travelled to Medina and converted to Islam and acquired the name Abdul Rasheed and was then known as Abdul Rasheed Quais. His family line carried on till approximately the fifteenth century when they left Afghanistan and settled in the North West Frontier Province in a village called Kalpaney in the area of Roh, which is why they are also known as the Rohilla Pathans. Maybe that's why my mother is such a *kunjoos* (miser) and finds certain incidents very amusing which, when told to me, I find very cruel and sadistic! She relates the following incident that happened with her Nana's (maternal grandfather) brother General Azimuddin Khan

Left to right: Zohra's maternal grandfather, Hamiduzzafar Khan and paternal grandfather, Kamadan Ataullah Khan

Zohra's maternal grand uncle General Azimuddin Khan, Regent of Rampur state

who was Commander-in-Chief of the Rampur Army: "Once on a *shikar* [hunting] visit to the Terai forest, Lord and Lady Connaught were invited by the General to accompany him. After semi-wounding a tiger, the General asked my mother's uncle and his cousin to show their Pathan prowess by teasing the wounded tiger with sticks—a most dangerous feat which the boys had to obey!"

Both her parents were from Rampur, they were cousins whose ancestor was Nawab Najibuddaulah (1708–1770). Her mother's side belonged to the Najibabad state but they later settled in Rampur. In 1857, the Nawab of Najibabad was Mehmood Khan who was against the British. He ran away to Bhopal, leaving his younger brother, Nawab Jalaluddin Khan, on the throne of Najibabad. When the British army came to this region, they shot him. His young widow, sons and daughters escaped in a bullock cart, taking all the family Oudh jewellery with them with the intention of going to Moradabad where my mother's grand uncle General Azimuddin Khan (the 'Tiger Teaser') was an army officer. Being in purdah they were at a loss as to where and when Moradabad was to come for they kept travelling for days on end in a forest because of the rampant mutiny all round. They finally settled in Moradabad.

In Rampur state they owned Angoori Bagh Palace, which has a lovely *hauz* (water tank) in it. General Azimuddin Khan once threw his five-year-old niece into the tank, ordering her to swim, which she did to save her life and later became a very good swimmer! It was General Azimuddin Khan's granddaughter who married the Nawab of Rampur state. My mother's paternal grandfather, though not of royal lineage, was a very rich man whose family owned two palaces known as Do Mehela. The area was known as Muhalla do-Mehela in Rampur. He inherited these palaces as well as a large amount of property from his stepmother. My grandfather would relate to my mother how they always had two elephants tied in the palace compound. As children he and his cousin brother would pluck off the pearl buttons from their father's *chogha* (cloak) while he was asleep and sell them in the market to buy sweets! Ammi hardly stayed in Rampur and only went there for weddings and other family gatherings.

I find it strange that, in this day and age, she is very proud of being *khandani* (belonging to an aristocratic family) and a Pathan and this fact has been instilled in by her forefathers. According to my mother, in marriages and matchmaking, "*Haddi aur khoon dekha jata tha*" (ancestory is seen). In other words, it would be the same as the Hindu caste system when marriages were decided upon by family background and upbringing. Ancestors were carefully examined with a keen eye. She also feels that too much of inter-marriage is not good, especially among the Muslims where a cousin can marry another cousin.

Many people have branded her as 'arrogant' and she thinks that this is because of her upbringing and the influence of her elder brother who taught her to never forget that she is *khandani*; to always be honest; never be afraid of anything or anyone and always work with courage. She says that Pathans are famous for two things—stubbornness and courage. Earlier in battle, when their men died and their bodies were just strewn on the battlefield, it was the women, the Pathanis, who would bury their dead.

Acting in a play for the students of Jamia Millia Islamia

On 27 April 2011, Ammi was ninety-nine, although she is still running on eighteen or is it sixteen! She is quite unbelievable and let me tell you she is also quite mad. Thank God for that. I am talking about Zohra Segal who happens to be my mother. Most of the time I think of her as a friend and only in my reflective moments do I think of her as my mother.

Zohra's mother, Natiqua Begum, who died when she was just seven-and-a-half years old

EARLY DAYS

Till today, whenever Ammi is playing with a kid, it is always her who becomes the 'child' in their little game and the kid she is playing with becomes the parent, elder sister or some voice of authority. My mother enjoys this. I have often wondered, is it because of a missed childhood? Or a craving for a mother whom she lost when she was only seven-and-a-half years old?

It was her mother who sent the sisters to boarding school at Queen Mary's College, Lahore. Ammi entered Queen Mary's on 19 October 1919 when she was seven years old and her mother was still alive. When the three sisters came home for their Christmas holidays, their mother died in January 1920 after giving birth to her youngest daughter who was just forty days old. Initially it was the eldest sister, Hajrah and my mother Zohra who were in the boarding school and then gradually all the five sisters were sent to the same place. At school they were known as Sahibzadi Hajrah Begum and Sahibzadi Zohra Begum. Their mother, whose name was Natiqua Begum, was known as Nabban bi.

My mother was and is very stubborn—as a child while trying to cut *supari* (betel nut), she picked up a *silbuta* (grinding stone), much against her mother's wishes. In the process she cut the tip of the third finger of her left hand. Blood oozed out and a little bit of flesh hung on but her mother was quick in realising what had happened and immediately cleaned the wound and put the bit of flesh back. The mark is still there and you can see it clearly in her fingerprint. She remembers her mother's words: "*Nakhoon se kabhi mat khujao, nakhoon ke neechey zeher hota hai*" (Never scratch with your nails, beneath them there is nothing but poison). Even now when Ammi cuts her nails she remembers her mother! Nani (maternal grandmother) was a very beautiful woman with flowing long black hair, and in my mother's memory she always wore a "*dheela* [loose] pyjama, kurta and dupatta". She thinks she always wore white, or perhaps her "*dheela* pyjama" was always white and since she barely came up to her thighs she just remembers the 'white'.

Nani was terrified of lizards (a trait that has been handed down to all of us) and Nana, who was a very good 'shot', would shoot down these creatures with mud pellets from his gun. At present my mother brings them down with empty plastic bottles! Nani was full of fun, laughter and song...In the afternoons when she used to rest the *farshi pankha* would be swaying and cooling the room (these were large fans hung from the ceiling with a strong rope attached to them which finished outside the room in the hands of a male attendant whose sole duty was to tug slowly and constantly at the rope so that the fan would sway and create a gentle breeze). Ammi and her brother and sister would blow on their mother's 'tummy' turn by turn and make her laugh. They would say, "*Ab hamari bari hai, ab hamari bari hai*" (Now it's my turn, now it's my turn)! She still remembers the stretch marks on her mother's stomach and the colour of her skin as being very fair. But, alas, she died after giving birth to her seventh child. Ammi's father, Mohammad Mumtazullah Khan, brought up his seven children single-handedly. He married for the second time after ten long years when his sisters insisted, but his second wife also passed away in childbirth.

Mohammad Mumtazullah Khan, Zohra's father, who single-handedly brought up the children after his wife's death

Ammi's father was a great inspiration in her life. He was a just man who always saw both sides of a situation and because of this trait the British, under whom he was employed, always sent him to quell Hindu-Muslim riots. This quality was amply demonstrated when my father (a Hindu) went to him to ask for my mother's hand in marriage. Nana was very upset, to which my father said that he was ready to become a Muslim. But Nana would have none of it. Instead, he said, "How do you think I would feel if my daughter became a Hindu!" Although initially he was against my parents getting married, he later became great friends with my father. This used to happen when Ammi was touring with Prithvi Theatres and both father-in-law and son-in-law would come down to meet her. During these sessions my father would cook fish for Nana and the two of them would finish it over a couple of drinks.

The Prithvi Theatres group in the 1950s—seen in the picture with Zohra are Prithviraj, Shashi and Jennifer Kapoor. Facing page: A sketch by Zohra of the time when she used to go hunting with her father

My grandfather was very strict with the upbringing of his children, to the extent that he even scolded my mother for putting *surma* (collyrium) in her eyes when she was a schoolgirl. Yet, although disappointed, he abided by her initial decision of not wanting to marry. One day he called her aside and gave her what he had saved up for her trousseau—a suitcase made of crocodile leather and a leopard skin coat. He had shot both the animals! My mother and some of her other brothers and sisters would sometimes go hunting with him. As Deputy Collector, he would have to go on Government tours and at times the kids were taken with him. They had a wonderful time living in canvas tents. Dried grass was put on the ground and then covered with mattresses for them to sleep on. When their father was busy they would run into the farms and eat sugarcane and *boot* (raw chickpea) and also watch with great interest how *gud* (jaggery) was made from sugarcane.

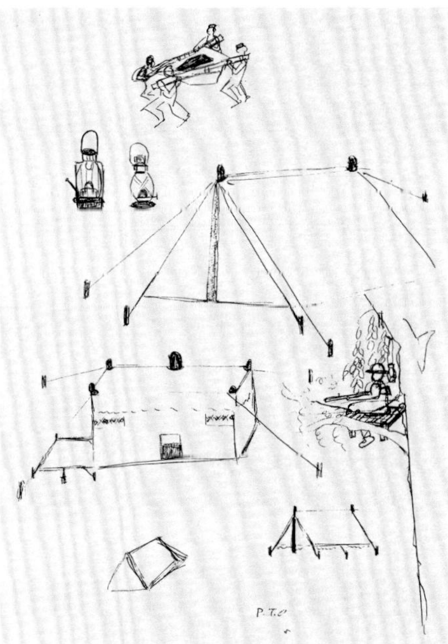

Nana was six feet tall, dark and had a very good physique. His skin explained a 'smallpox' attack in his childhood. My mother never thought that he was a good looking man, but, whenever he went to fetch his daughters from Dalhousie for the holidays, some of the teachers would swoon at his looks! He definitely had an impressive presence. Till the age of sixty he kept up with all his fitness exercises. Very punctual, he would always go to the railway station two hours before time. Ammi is the same; if she is to travel, attend a function or get-together, it is a nightmare for those with her! She will have her clothes taken out the previous day, her shoes/sandals, her handbag and handkerchief and so on. Another quality that she has imbibed from him is of being very methodical and particular about the whys and wherefores of her possessions. If you ask her for a safety pin or a needle she will guide you to the innermost 'secret places' in her cupboard or dressing table drawer and lo and behold there it will be!

Always tastefully dressed, her father's suits and sherwanis were beautifully tailored and his shoes were custom-made. He was fond of singing and also played the sitar. His favourite was Ghalib's '*Yeh na thi hamari kismat...*' (It was not my destiny...), which he would hum every now and then. Once my mother composed a song and sang it to him and he immediately said, "This is very good. It's *Raag* Malkauns." The song was:

> *Din sawan ke, aur jhoola na dala ri*
> *Kaisi kahoon ay ri sakhi, piya pardes ri*
> *Jhoola na dala ri*
> *Surma na lago mori ankhiyan, missi na lago morey honth*
> *Nangi lago mori baiyan, churiyan na pehni ri*
> *Din sawan ke, jhoola na dala ri*
> (O friend, the monsoons are here and the swings are not hung!
> My beloved is away!
> My eyes are without collyrium
> My lips aren't sweet
> My arms are bare without their bangles
> The monsoons are here and the swings are not hung
> O friend, my beloved is away!)

GROWING UP

Queen Mary's College was founded by an English woman, Miss Western, in 1908 in Lahore. Although it was a school it was called a 'college', but after my mother left, graduation classes were introduced. For the first twenty years, only girls from 'aristocratic' families were given admission. It is a double-storeyed red brick building shaped like a three-sided rectangle, which the girls would call *choolah* (stove). It has fountains in the centre, surrounded by cyprus trees and flanked by tennis courts. There were also four badminton courts and a huge ground which was a netball field that later served as a hockey field. On one side of the badminton courts were the quarters for the Indian staff members and on the other side was a small hospital. Among the Indian staff was an Anglo-Indian matron called Sisterji who would perpetually tell the students, "I want my girls to go into the world and be like flowers." This invariably

Acting in Kenilworth, *a play that was staged when Zohra was in Queen Mary's College, Lahore*

brought a smile to their faces. *Unsey bahut seekha hamney* (we learnt a lot from her), remembers Ammi. The central portion of the *choolah* had classrooms on the ground floor and dormitories on the first floor. On the right of the rectangle, on the ground floor, were the office and quarters of the Principal Miss Cox and also the quarters of some of the British staff, while the other staff members had rooms on the first floor as well.

My mother had several British teachers and she often speaks of them quite fondly. Miss Lloyd Harvey, her favourite, was a Scottish woman who taught them English. Then there was Miss Comozzy, whose name meant 'gardener' in Italian. Since the girls were such snobs, they were horrified to think that they were being taught by a gardener's daughter! Then there was Miss NJ Toogood whom they all dreaded and called her "naughty-junglee". She was very strict. But, when my mother got typhoid, it was Miss Toogood who went and stayed with her and nursed her back to good health. My mother became very fond of her and in later years they used to correspond regularly, with her addressing my mother as 'babe' and signing off as 'dragon'. Miss Harrison, who my mother thinks was Anglo-Chinese, was also very fond of her and called her 'you dear,

Miss Christian, Zohra's teacher, dressed as a pahadi *(person living in the mountains)*

dear Chinese'. One of the Indian matrons would refer to my mother as 'pretty zampha'. Ammi corresponded regularly with Miss Harvey, Miss Toogood and Miss Harrison and even met them in 1962 when she went to England. Another teacher she remembers is Miss Humphrey, a beautiful English woman who was their Art teacher and on whom all the girls had a 'crush'! Ammi's friend Mumtaz Shahnavaz, who was a day boarder, used to bring violets and narcissi from her garden for my mother. But the little girl Zohra would creep up to Miss Humphrey's room in the evening, just as she was dressing up for dinner and give them to her shyly and awkwardly through the *chik* (blinds). Miss Humphrey's response—"Oh how nice, thank you!" would make my mother's day.

In school, Ammi had two double promotions and therefore reached the tenth class very soon, at the age of fifteen in 1927. In those days they started their first standard when they were just seven. Miss Cox kept her there for two more years, saying that if she'd let her go, her family would just marry her off! When I asked my mother what she did for those two years, she chuckled and said, "I had a hell of a time and won the Lady Hailey's Silver Cup for being the 'Best All Rounder' for two years, but, when I took the final examination, I scraped through in third division."

In summer the school would go to Dalhousie for three months every year. Their classes would be held in the open under the apricot trees. It was here, during one of her initial trips, that she witnessed a snowfall. She learnt about different flowers which she had never seen in the plains such as rhododendrons, lily of the valley, white violets, hydrangea, larkspur and balsam.

There were thousands of daisies spread all over the hillside. The children also got to know that a four-leaf clover was lucky and so they would spend hours looking for it. Ammi found quite a few!

The Science teacher, Miss Cohen, taught them two French songs: *'Ces les rats, ces les rats...'* and *'Frere Jacques...'* Miss Cohen once put a hair of the stinging nettle under a microscope and showed it to the girls. My mother couldn't believe her eyes as she witnessed so much activity on that single hair.

Miss Toogood was a good walker and climber and it was she who arranged a trip twenty miles out to Khajjiar, which had a lake with a moving island. If it was a sunny day, the teachers would stop the classes and take them for a picnic to the neighbouring waterfalls. And, when the monsoons started around mid-June my mother would run and dance around in the compound despite the flashes of lightning, not paying heed to the frantic calls of the teachers to come in! She wouldn't listen to anyone and would loudly sing a ditty on the rain: "*Barso Ram dhadakey se,*

Teacher Miss NJ Toogood, whom the students dreaded as she was very strict

Chamba—the school would go to Dalhousie during the summer months

budhiya margaye faquey se..."

Due to this boarding school my mother's upbringing has been quite British. In fact, when the two of us are joking and fooling around I often tell her, *"Tum to galti se Hindustan mein payda ho gayein. Tumhe to* England *mein janam lena tha"*(By mistake you have taken birth in India, actually you should've been born in England). However, despite the teaching staff being British, and the fact that the history taught was British as well as the hymns sung ('All things bright and beautiful', 'Onwards,

Sandrigham Cottage, Dalhousie, where classes were often held in the open, under the apricot trees

onwards soldiers' and others), she learnt the piano and also the tabla. In addition, the students wore only Indian clothes, depending on which province they belonged to, except on Sports Day when they would all wear white kurta pyjama or salwar with a rose-colour dupatta. Tennis shoes were allowed for games and the Sports Day, otherwise they were made to wear only *chappal*s or *juttee*s (Indian footwear) and no ribbons, only *paranda*s (Indian braids), in the hair. Despite all this, she admits that she is nothing but an Anglicised snob; even now she dreams in English!

GIFTED CHILD

The 'actress' in my mother has been there since her first year in school when, at the age of seven-and-a-half, she was selected to enact the part of a lion in a play called *The Rose and The Ring*. She wore brown churidar pyjamas and had a brown doormat tied across her back. At the same time she had also won a prize for Urdu and, when she was getting dressed as a lion in the school office, her name was announced in the assembly; somebody rushed in and told her to run and receive her prize. Excitedly, the 'little lion' ran onto the stage, bringing down the house in fits of laughter! Prize Giving Day was a big occasion and her memory absolutely astounds me. She even remembers what she received—"It was a beautiful cane basket filled with brass toy vessels such as *belan, chakla, kadhai, kadhchi* and *thali*."

At the age of fourteen, when she was in Middle School, she won fifteen rupees as a prize for a painting of a coxcomb, which was displayed in an art exhibition in Lahore. She confesses with a giggle, "I just painted to get a prize and I think my Art teacher had touched it up here and there." With that money she bought a Kodak Baby Brownie box

A photograph taken by Zohra in Bhopal, using her Kodak Baby Brownie box camera

camera and took several photographs; some of these are still there in her album.

Another photograph taken by Zohra with the Kodak Baby Brownie box camera

Ammi was very keen to learn the *esraj* (stringed musical instrument) and singing. She says she was supposed to have a very good voice and then adds with laughter, "I don't know what happened?" As a schoolgirl she was very fond of singing and was always selected to sing the hymns with the others, so she wrote to her father to seek his permission to learn singing. Since this was a 'purdah school' no men were allowed within the premises, even the servants were all females. Strangely enough, the music teacher, who was living in Lahore, was a gentleman named Professor Gargi from Vishnu Digamber School in Mumbai. She learnt a lot of songs from him and of course we all have a good laugh when she sings them now. She also learnt the tabla from him. On one of their trips to Dalhousie she tied a string to the Brownie camera and sat in front of it, holding the *esraj* and the tabla. She somehow managed to pull the string and take a photograph of herself. My mother still wonders how Professor Gargi was allowed into her school to teach.

When the very first 'talkie' film, *Ben-Hur*, was shown in the Government College in Lahore (which was a boys' college), she had to write to her father to be allowed to watch it with a batch of girls from her school. The girls saw the film from behind a *sola chik* (a screen made out of *sola* plants); now all she remembers about *Ben-Hur* is the drumming when the slaves were made to row in the ships, she maintains that this made quite an impact on her! Incidentally, Prithviraj Kapoor was a student of this college.

THREE OF SEVEN

Nani and Nana had seven children and my mother was number three. She had an elder brother, an elder sister and a younger brother and three younger sisters. Out of these seven, her younger brother Ikramullah was her favourite, she loved him very much. When she was five years old, her 'Mamu' (uncle) adopted her and took her away to his home in Lucknow. Ikram missed her and would save sweets for her one by one, day after day and, when the container was full, he ate them all himself! Ammi finds this extremely funny! He was a Commodore in the Indian Navy in Mumbai and later migrated to Karachi after Partition. Her elder brother, Zakaullah, was an engineer who played an important role in the building of the Zakaria Bridge

The five sisters, from left to right: Uzra, Zohra, Sabra, Hajrah and Amina. Seated below: Kiran (left) and Salima, Hajrah's daughter (right)

Above and facing page: Practising in her cabin for Varsha Mangal

in Kolkata (then Calcutta) where he was posted by the Indian Government. Later he, too, migrated to Karachi and was the chief engineer of the Karachi Port Trust. Her eldest sister, Hajrah Begum, was a staunch Communist, a freedom fighter and the founder of the National Federation of Indian Women.

Ammi and her younger sister, Uzra, never wanted to go to Pakistan. In fact, my mother was shocked when both her brothers and her two youngest sisters opted for Pakistan! She was also amazed that some of her other relatives who had been born and brought up in India and who had their closest friends in this country opted for Pakistan. She thought that when

Pakistan was made all the 'mullahs' and 'maulavis' (Muslim teachers of religion) would settle there—little did she imagine that her two youngest sisters Amina (an ex-Santiniketan student and a double MA in Education from Leeds, UK) and Sabra (who had done a Physical Education course from London) as well as her two brothers would go there, especially as their upbringing was so secular and they had many dear friends among the Hindu community. She thought maybe it was the possibility of new opportunities in a new country. Her father also did not choose Pakistan and only went there after twenty long years and that too because his favourite daughter Uzra had to follow her husband.

With her younger sister, Uzra (left)

Actually Uzra's moving to Pakistan pained her a lot and although they had been together as young girls as dancers in Uday Shankar's troupe they had become very close only after my mother joined Prithvi Theatres in October 1945. During Uday Shankar's tours from 1936 to 1938, when her younger sister joined the troupe, they were together but never close. Ammi being the older one used to boss her a lot. Punctuality was of utmost importance during tours, especially as trains, buses and ships had to be caught on time. My mother would (and still does) keep her alarm clock five minutes fast. Since the sisters were sharing a room, Ammi would get ready and scold Uzra Khala (Aunt) for not getting ready! Uzra Khala resented

February 1937: On the way to America—Zohra and Uzra seen with Ravi Shankar, Uday Shankar, Simkie and others

Clockwise from above: Prague, 1936; the Dartington Hall group; Zohra with Kathakali dancer Madhavan Nair; returning from Bali with Uday Shankar and Kamala Chowdhury, 1938. Facing page, clockwise from top left: Zohra with Uday Shankar at the Raja Rani Temple, Bhubaneswar, Odisha; Uday Shankar in Gandhar; the Uday Shankar troupe in Budapest, 1936

Clockwise from top left: Zohra with Simkie and Ravi Shankar; with Michael Chekov in Dartington Hall (photograph taken by Uday Shankar); with Uzra in Varsha Mangal; *with Simkie in* Rashik, *1935*

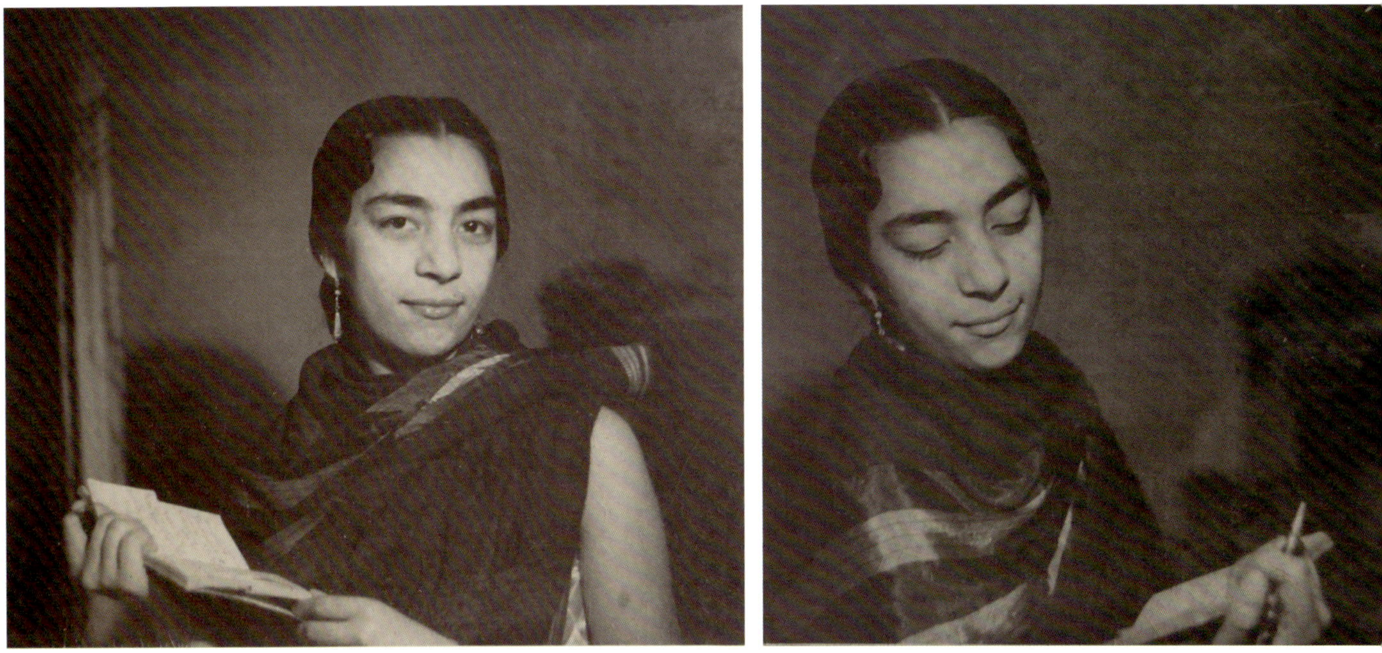

Zohra in the 1930s

this, but half-way through the 'coast-to-coast' tour of America, she found out about the clock being fast and then onwards took her own sweet time to get ready.

Ammi held quite an important position in the troupe as 'Uday Shankar's partner after Simkie'; her younger sister was part of the group along with Madhavan Nair and 'Robu' (Ravi Shankar). Ammi laughingly remembers how, whenever something would come out in the papers, she would always ask Uzra: "*Dekho, dekho, mere barey mein kuch nikla hai*?" (Is there something about me?) She confesses that she was very full of herself, to which I retort, "Well, you still are like that!" During her Prithvi Theatres days, she used to take one corner in the make-up room at Opera House and nobody dared to touch any of her belongings, not even my aunt Uzra, who was actually Prithviraj

Clockwise from top left: With Mr Spachek in Prague, 1936; in Prague; another mesmerising performance

Kapoor's (called 'Papaji') leading lady in most of the plays. 'Zohra di', as she was known in the theatre, was very particular about her make-up box, costume and jewellery due to her training with Uday Shankar. In spite of my mother's position and dominating nature, Ammi feels that people remember Uzra more than her because of her exceptional beauty and, hence Ammi developed a complex and tried very hard to be charming and attract attention. Personally I feel my aunt had a sweeter and more amiable nature. My mother till today remembers a comment when, after a performance in America, someone came backstage to meet them and asked for 'Miss Mumtaz'. The doorman near their dressing room queried, "Which one; the one with the big eyes or the one with the big hips?"

In 1936 the Uday Shankar troupe had made Dartington Hall in the UK its base with two other famous groups—The Kurt Jose Ballet and Michael Chekov's training centre known as the Barn

Left to right: Zohra in the 1930s; with Uzra and Ikram

Theatre. Michael Chekov, known as 'Misha', in spite of having a very beautiful wife, would make Uzra Khala sit near him and say in broken English, "I can't help it, she does something to me!" While touring England with Uday Shankar, the BBC requested a publicity appearance by the Uday Shankar dance troupe for its new television programme. This took place at the Alexandria Palace in London and Ammi remembers the unusual make-up they had to apply—pale green for the face and purple for the lips! The performing area was barely three feet by four feet where they danced two items—a solo by Uday Shankar and *Snanam* by Simkie, Zohra and Uzra. This was also the year that Prince Edward of Great Britain abdicated the throne.

And though Ammi joined Uday Shankar first and Khala came later; it was the other way around with Prithvi Theatres.

Zohra with Kameshwar Segal, whom she married in August 1942

TWO SISTERS

My parents, who were running their own dance school on Empress Road in Lahore called Zoresh Dance Institute, found it very difficult to carry on their profession due to the impending Partition of India as they were a Hindu-Muslim couple! Khala, who had left the Uday Shankar Almora Centre and was married to the actor-writer Hamid Butt, was now settled in Mumbai. She was the leading lady of Prithviraj Kapoor in his theatre, which she had joined in 1944. She wrote to my parents in Lahore and suggested they come to Mumbai and try their luck in films. Since my father was the art director in a film starring Suraiya and was also winding up the affairs of the Zoresh Dance Institute, he had to stay on in Lahore and join my mother later in Mumbai. My parents stayed with my aunt and uncle, sharing their tiny flat in 41 Pali Hill, which they, in turn, were sharing with Chetan Anand and his wife Uma, Dev Anand

Conducting dance lessons at Empress Road, Lahore

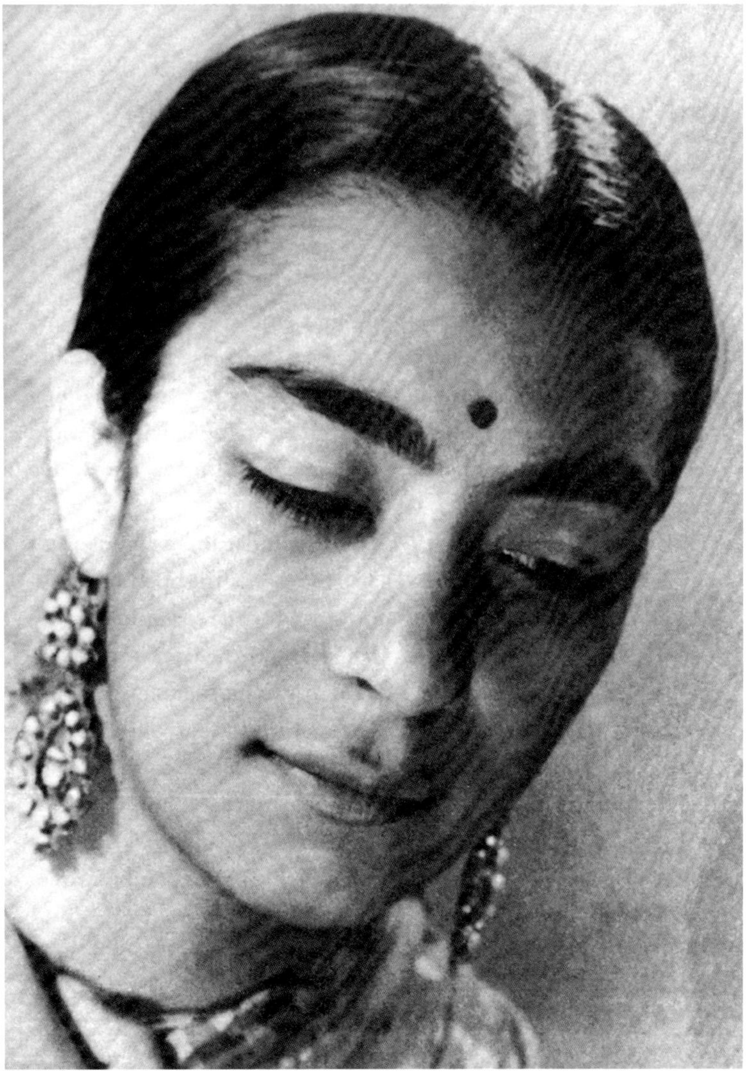

Zohra in Budapest, 1937

and Vijay Anand. Ammi still remembers Dev Uncle (as we kids used to call him) standing in front of a mirror, brushing his hair and asking her, "Didi, do you think they'll take me as a hero?" My mother also remembers Chetan Uncle and Uma Aunty's kindness in allowing them to share their flat.

With Uzra in Juhu, Mumbai, 1935; top: the sisters in the 'Pathan' group

After some time my aunt and uncle shifted to Soona Mahal on Marine Drive, Churchgate and, as soon as the lower two floors got vacated, my parents and I moved downstairs. In the initial years Ammi was offered roles in films where the director would want her to wear a swimming costume and emerge from a rose bowl! With her background and training she was nothing but horrified by this proposal. Of course she refused, but my father kept up with his art direction in films. My aunt, who was in Prithvi Theatres, would take my mother with her to the rehearsals and shows. The first play she saw (and was not very impressed) was *Shakuntala*. But when she saw *Deewar*, she fell in love with it and later joined the theatre first as dance-director and then as an actress. From then onwards both sisters were together for fourteen long years.

Emotionally and financially my aunt was a great support to my mother. She was better off than my parents as she was the leading lady of Prithvi Theatres and also my uncle, who although never had a regular job, earned a lot from his writing, film scripting and gambling! Since they had no children my

Kameshwar Segal was a noted dancer and choreographer

Uzra in Prithvi Theatres' Gaddar

aunt would spoil us quite a bit, never saying 'no' to anything we wanted. She once confessed to my mother that she had become so fond of my younger brother Pavan that she had thought of adopting him, but gave up the idea since it would cause a lot of pain. She was so generous and gracious towards us that one never felt obliged to her in any way. My father was very fond of her. After my father's death it was my aunt who kept all three of us at her place on Marine Drive.

Whenever they went for a reception with Papaji, the ladies would always ask her about his leading lady (that is, Khala) and my mother would give them all the information about her. They would ask who she was; to this Ammi replied that she was her sister and they would turn around and say, "*Sagi*!" (real). She now says that she could have slapped them for that comment. The strange thing is that both of them looked very different in their youth and now Khala is mistaken for my mother on many occasions.

Since a decade there has been a great reunion between the sisters due to the play *Ek Thi Naani* (Once There Was a Granny)

Zohra joined Prithvi Theatres as a dance-director and went on to become an actress with the group

in which they performed together for the first time after thirty-three years. It has been written by a Pakistani playwright, Shahid Nadeem. They have performed this play with Ajoka Theatre and their artists in India, Pakistan and London. The story has been inspired from the two sisters' lives and is a great hit with audiences on both sides of the 'border' and elsewhere. For the two of them it was like re-living their theatre touring/dancing/performing days.

UNCLE MEMPHIS

There are several incidents revolving round my mother's Mamu (maternal uncle) Sahibzada Saiduzzafar Khan, whom I used to call 'Memphis'. One that my mother relates is of the time when he was sitting on the roof of their house with his Chacha, the General, and the latter said, "If you are a real Pathan you will jump down with the chair you are sitting in." The boy obeyed to show his courage, breaking almost all the bones in his body in the process! Perhaps it was this incident that inspired Memphis to become the foremost surgeon in India and the first Indian principal of the Lucknow Medical College. All the surgeons I met later in life had been his students.

His visits to his sister's home were great as he would bring my mother and her brother and sister wonderful toys. In those days my mother's toys were dolls made of cloth, a mud cart, which when pulled would make sounds, a *phirki* (paper fan) or wooden toys. Memphis would get them dolls with blue eyes and blonde hair as well as plasticine to mould and make things. According to my mother, he was "very tall and very fair, just like a Pathan. Sometimes he would put

Zohra's maternal uncle, Sahibzada Saiduzzafar Khan, also known as Memphis

Zohra in the 1930s

one kid on each shoulder and one on his head and walk! He was full of fun!" His first child was a boy, Mahmud. Later he had a girl who died at a very young age. "My aunt would cry and was totally heartbroken after this tragedy," narrates Ammi. "I was a naughty child and he became very fond of me. It was then that they decided to adopt me. So when I was just five years old he took me to Lucknow by train and of course he always travelled first class! I was in Lucknow for a few months. Mahmud, who was a few years older than me, was also there. He was a lovely looking child, very fair." My mother was colour conscious and considered herself to be attractive as a child, but never a beauty. Mahmud would often tease her about her looks. Her uncle and aunt would go off to Nainital in summer, to Oak Cottage, which according to my mother is still there. She says her uncle was her hero and nobody could be more clever, more funny or with a better sense of humour than him! His wife, who was a simple lady, was perpetually being teased by father and son, which at times became a "bit too much". Her Mamu chucked up his job as the principal of the Lucknow Medical College because they were paying him a lower salary than the previous principal who had been an Englishman. He had enough money and pride to be able to do that! Later in his life he became a minister in Bhopal state.

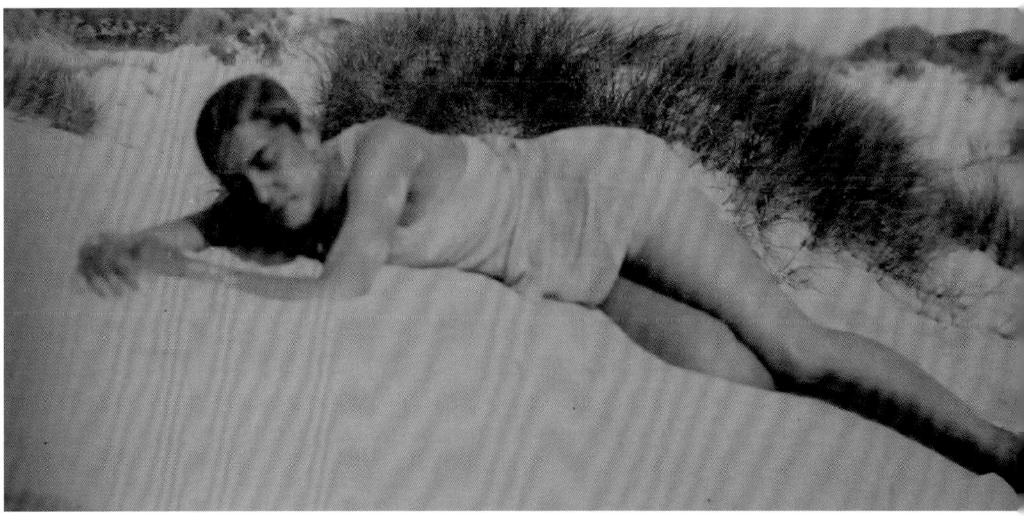

Enjoying the beach, 1930s

In Nainital, Ammi and the servant would go to Mahmud's school to fetch him. Here, there was an area where broken ink-pots made of porcelain were thrown. Till today Ammi regrets that she could never find an unbroken ink-pot, which would have made a beautiful 'potty' for her doll! Sometimes Mahmud was a little mean to her—once he made her sit on a pony and then whipped the animal that ran wild with this terrified five-year-old on its back!

After some months Nani started missing her daughter and Ammi had to go back to the plains when they came to fetch her. Also, Mahmud was then packed off to Sherborne, a public school in England. After two years Ammi was sent to boarding

Saiduzzafar Khan's house in Dehradun, Nasreen, now Welham Girls' School—a sketch by Zohra

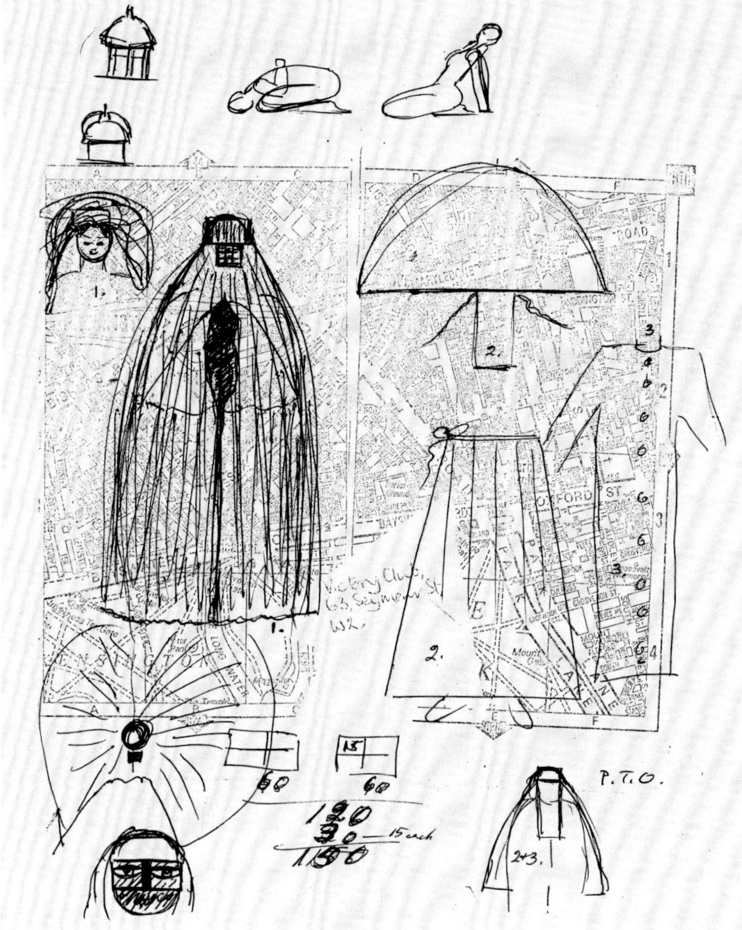

Memories of her road journey to Europe—sketch by Zohra

school in Lahore, but she never lost touch with her uncle. She would visit them or vice versa and even write to him, though perhaps not as regularly as she wrote to her father. She wrote in English as her Urdu was bad because their school was very British and they were more influenced by the Punjabi culture than that of Uttar Pradesh. She is quite embarrassed when she admits, "My father-in-law, although a Hindu, wrote and spoke better Urdu than me!" She also tells me that during rehearsals in the Prithvi Theatres, Papaji would often be surprised by the bad Urdu pronunciation of the two sisters, considering they were from Rampur.

Originally Ammi wanted a career in order to escape marriage. She sought her father's permission to become the first girl pilot in India (an idea given to her by her brother). She was still in school and he wrote back saying that she could but if something happened to her he would never be able to forgive himself. This brought tears to her eyes and she gave up the idea. But her other passion was acting.

Ammi was very keen to go abroad. In those days the idea of studying abroad and getting a degree from there meant a lot. Also, in the words of her teacher, Miss Harvey, in Queen Mary's, upon seeing her act, "If this child were in England she

In the convertible Dodge, just before leaving for Europe by car

More sketches by Zohra on some childhood memories

would be earning ten pounds a week on the stage", helped her to make up her mind.

At first her father was reluctant to send her alone to England to study at the tender age of eighteen. Then, at the family conference, he said he would agree if she was betrothed to Mahmud who was studying at Oxford. However, her Mamu was absolutely against this idea and did not want either of the young ones to be tied down in this manner. He wrote to her and told her that there were two ways in which she could travel to England—with one of her uncles, Sir Abdussamad Khan, the then Chief Minister of Rampur state (who was going to England to attend some Princes' Conference) in a luxury liner as his secretary or by car (a convertible Dodge) with him. He also warned her that it would be a long, tiring and tough journey.

Ammi agreed to the second option because her Mamu was her hero and because of the adventure that was in store. Little did she realise that every bone in her body would be crying out for mercy owing to the constant road travel from 8 am to 8 pm with stops only for meals.

The others who accompanied them on this trip were a mechanic called Muqueem and a young nephew of her uncle's friend, Wahid, who wanted a ride up to Basra in Iraq. They started this journey in the four-seater Dodge in September 1930 from Dehradun, where the entire family had gathered to say goodbye. Ammi wore jodhpurs and a cotton top that had been especially tailored for her as well as a Kashmiri jacket. A sola hat, which she never wore, also accompanied her. She had very short hair, as it had been cut during the time she had typhoid, from which she had just recovered.

With Simkie, the driver and Nikova, Dead Sea, Palestine, 1936

Having fun with Simkie, Palestine

The car had a trailer attached and off they went from Dehradun to Lahore, then on to Multan and Ziarat at a height of 9,000 feet, where the political agent working for the British Government, Sherbat Khan, lived! As they arrived at his camp for lunch the first thing that caught their eye was a table lined with all the sherbets that one could think of! Ammi could not stop giggling and her uncle had a hard time trying to control his laughter. The compensation was Sherbat Khan's very handsome son on whom Ammi developed an immediate crush!

Zohra had been very keen to visit the Dead Sea, which, according to her, looked like pink blotting paper with ink spots all over

From there on to Quetta, where there was a very steep climb and sharp turns. The trailer broke down near Fort Munroe and had to be disbanded. One day, while the car was being taken to the service station, a woman who spoke broken Urdu came into Ammi's room and became quite chatty. Ammi was happy to talk and rattled away about her life quite innocently. When she related the incident to her uncle, his expression changed and he warned her about the danger of talking to strangers. Sure enough, when they left Quetta (which was the last post in British India), a hefty young man with dark glasses followed them right up to Baluchistan. On enquiring, her uncle found out that he was a rascal notorious for abducting girls.

In Baluchistan they met with a heavy sandstorm, which darkened everything. The car shook with the force of the wind and Ammi was really frightened. She says these sandstorms were killers known for uprooting everything. Even though the car was turned around and the windows sealed, the sand got into their sandwiches! When it subsided they went to Nushki, a small town in Baluchistan, to rest for a while. It was a clear, full moon night. Ammi lay down on the grass and saw the moon through her binoculars—an experience she still cherishes with awe and wonder.

The next day they travelled to Dalbandine to collect the previously ordered petrol, which was brought down by rail from Duzdab in what was then known as Waziristan. Then on to Meshed in Iran where she had her first proper bath; so far they had to make do with just a little water and sponging! The nights were spent in *serais* (place for the accommodation of travellers), sleeping on carpets, with bugs for company. There was a toilet built for her under one of the back seats of the Dodge and the men used the desert! Owing to a scarcity of water, travelling conditions were pretty bad until they reached Meshed. Her uncle cooked for the two of them in an Ick-Mick cooker. Cooking was done on a gas stove by placing one container on top of the other and the final edible product was very bland, with salt being added for taste!

This first bath was in a *hamam* (bathing retreat). Ammi had to strip in front of a very fat naked woman (an experience she can never forget) who bathed all the women. She had to go through deep stone *hamams*, which started from very cold to very hot. The fat assistant kept rubbing Ammi till she thought her skin would come off! In India, my mother had been used to coconut oil shampoo and had, therefore, carried some with her on this trip. When she took the bottle to the *hamam* to shampoo her hair, the assistant was so excited to see it, as she had never seen anything like it, that she nearly spilled half of it while applying it on my mother's head and then on her own! When this traumatic experience was over and Ammi was dressed, she was put on a stone slab to rest and she remembers dozing off for what seemed like hours of heavenly sleep.

After Meshed everything changed. Iran was beautiful with delicious fruits, pulaos, Persian cuisine, early morning sounds of Bhairavi music played on the Persian lute, the climate and the comfort of a proper bed with sheets and pillows. Here onwards they stayed in good hotels. Ammi recalls that during winter the poor children just wrapped themselves in naan (in Persia the naans were huge) at night and went off to sleep while on the streets the women were seen in the latest Parisian clothes. Yet others wore burkhas, also called *char shaf* (four folds). They then travelled on to Tehran, Isfahan and Shiraz, which is the birthplace of the famous poet Saadi. Ammi was shocked to see nothing except a donkey roaming in a deserted field! What she found really funny all through Persia was that her uncle, who prided himself in his knowledge of the Persian language, was not understood by anybody in that country. They mostly spoke French or a Persian which was very different from his.

From Shiraz they went down to Basra to leave Wahid for his studies and then on to Al Najaf, Karbala, Babylon and finally Baghdad, the capital of Iraq. Here they stayed for quite some days, almost a week, in the Haram *serai* of the *mufti*, the head of the Muslim religion. It was an honour to be invited by the *mufti* and although Ammi could not speak Arabic she got on quite well with the women. She remembers the breakfast as being rich and difficult to digest—it was parathas and eggs. The coffee was thick, excessively sweet and without milk. From here the journey was treacherous and dangerous because they had to cross the Arabian Desert in forty-eight hours of non-stop driving. There were several other tourists who were also crossing with them and the entire convoy was given army escort from fear of an attack by bandits. They reached their

Dressed like an Arabic woman, Baghdad

destination, Beirut, and the much awaited sea which Ammi had never seen before. "It looked like pink blotting paper with ink spots all over," she recalls. Here they were met by two other members, one was her cousin Mahmud and the other Aunty Dicta (Benedicta Haslund), her uncle's Norwegian girlfriend whom he had met when he was studying surgery at Edinburgh.

Mahmud found my mother very funny with her purdah school background and the way in which she spoke English. He, of course, had been studying in Oxford! Since they were thrown a lot together he would tease her with the following poem that really annoyed Ammi:

The flowers that bloom in the spring tra laa!

Have nothing to do with the case

For I have under my wing tra laa!

The most preposterous thing tra laa!

With the caricature of a face, tra laa!

With the caricature of a face, tra laa!

With the caricature of a face, tra laa!

From Beirut they went to Balbek, Damascus, Jerusalem, the Dead Sea, along the beach of Acra, reaching Nazareth (the birthplace of Jesus Christ) on 25 December 1930. Then on to Egypt where they went to Cairo, experienced the Valley of the Kings, the Pyramids, the Sphinx, the tomb of Tutankhamen, inside the Pyramid and Alexandria. Here they left the car and their mechanic who, in their absence, became a sought after dentist for pulling out the teeth of the local Egyptians with his pliers! Then they took a boat down the river Nile to

Dresden, East Germany, 1933—Zohra attended the Mary Wigman Dance School here

Luxor. From Luxor her uncle went further down to the Lotus Temple of Aswaan, leaving my mother, her cousin and Aunty Dicta to return to Alexandria by boat. Later all three went to Dresden, Germany where Ammi joined the Mary Wigman Dance School.

Kameshwarnath Segal—he dropped the 'nath' later; his daughter, Kiran, referred to him as 'Dost'

DEAR 'DOST'

My father (I used to refer to him as 'Dost') came with the first batch of students to the Almora Centre in March 1940. He was a student of painting from the Arts College in Indore, spoke very good Urdu and dressed smartly. Every month the students would present some of their works in dance or painting. My father was also a classmate of the renowned painter MF Husain. But, he had come to the Uday Shankar Centre to learn dance. At one such student's exhibition he had taken fungus from the pine trees, collaged it on to paper and painted paddy fields beneath. He named this work 'Burmese Huts'. Ammi was fascinated by this exhibit. She felt that if this young boy had

Zohra and Kameshwar at their marriage, August 1942

Zohra and Kameshwar in The Lotus Dance, *choreographed by Kameshwar, Lahore, 1945*

been sent abroad to study further he would have become a great painter. Later, when Ammi met MF Husain in Delhi, he told her, "When Segal and I were studying I was one of the backbenchers compared to him."

Apart from being a well-known dancer, my mother was one of the most popular teachers at the Almora Centre and apparently this attracted my father to her. However, at this time he was in love with a very attractive girl—Sundari Shridharani—now Director, Triveni Kala Sangam, New Delhi. Ammi had been invited to Lucknow to give a talk on her life and when it was being broadcast live, everybody at the Centre listened, but my father was literally glued to the radio.

Romance blossomed during the creation of the Ramlila shadow play. My father was appointed to design the costumes and masks and my mother was assisting him. Unfortunately, the monkey masks were very uncomfortable and gave the dancers a lot of trouble during the rehearsals. That was when my father designed a novel mask, which allowed the dancers to see and breathe comfortably. A third-year student, Jitendra Guloy, who had been appointed to help in fetching colours, dyes, paint brushes, dusters and so on, was always hanging around with them and the young lovers were unable to be alone. As time went by, their relationship became stronger and they decided to get married. Initially, Ammi was not for it. She kept reminding my father that he was so much younger than her, that he was a Hindu and she a Muslim and although neither of them believed in these differences, she said their families would be offended. My father would have none of it and so they took leave to get married and then resumed their work at the Centre.

A student of art, Kameshwar went to the Uday Shankar Centre, Almora, to exhibit his paintings and then later to learn dance

When her in-laws received a telegram about my parents' decision to get married, Chachaji (my paternal grandfather) sat with the telegram and Baua (my paternal grandmother) asked him what it was. He informed her that his son was marrying the infamous Muslim dancer from the Uday Shankar troupe. Baua apparently said, "So what, if he has made her the queen of his heart then she is the queen of this house." After the wedding, when they went to Sanavad in Madhya Pradesh to meet them, my mother reminisces, "From the first day my mother-in-law made me sit customarily in the *chauka* (kitchen)." The tradition in the Segal family was that everybody sat together to eat in the *chauka*. Each one would sit with their thali in front of them. Mangal, the tailor's son and Bharosey, the servant boy whom my grandmother had picked up from somewhere, also sat with them. For quite some time my father and his brothers thought that these two were their brothers. My grandmother was very orthodox and would never take a paan from anyone but, on the very first day, she made my mother eat from the same thali as my grandfather. She was almost illiterate and could only read the Gurmukhi script of the Radha Soami sect and that, too, with some difficulty. Oddly enough, when she would visit us in Pali Hill, she would come to our room in the afternoon and ask my mother to read out stories of Oscar Wilde to her. Patiently, Ammi would translate each story. Her favourite was *The Rose and the Nightingale*.

Chachaji was very fond of singing and at any given opportunity would bring out the harmonium and start singing. Apparently, he knew all the songs from the Parsi theatre, songs written by Agha Hashar. My grandmother, whose name was Charanadhari, was only thirteen when she got married. She had thirteen children of which only eight survived, that is, six brothers and two sisters. After my parents' marriage, my grandparents were exposed to Prithvi Theatres. So, one day my mother took her mother-in-law to see *Deewar* in which she plays a foreign woman, dressed in Western clothes, smoking and flirting. After it was over and they reached home, Ammi asked Baua what she thought of her *bahu* (daughter-in-law). Baua replied, "*Beti, tu lakh aadmiyon mein bhi khadi rahey, main teri nazar pehechanti hoon*"(Even if you stand among one lakh men, I know your true nature).

Recently, when Ammi spoke about her gurus at the Almora Centre—Guru Kandapa Pillai for Bharatnatyam, Guru Amobi Singh for Manipuri and Guru Shankaran Namboodiri from the Kala Mandalam for Kathakali—she said that Guru Shankaran Namboodiri used to say, "If Zohra was a man and I could speak English, we could conquer the world!" Speaking about Kathak, she said that Uday Shankar never thought very highly of this dance form and, therefore, did not include it in their training courses. Guru Amobi Singh's advice to the students would be, "Even in dirt if you find a piece of gold—take it!"

The day my parents got married in Tagore Town, Allahabad, very few people turned up for the wedding. Ammi remembers how the whole country was in turmoil because of the Quit India movement. India had rebelled and wanted the British out. There were American GIs with their stenguns at the railway station and curfew was in force from 7 pm. The registration of the wedding took place at home and the reception was held in a hotel in Allahabad.

Taking part in a dance ballet on Shiva and Parvati, Lawrence Gardens, Lahore, 1944

Her share of her mother's jewellery had been sold to a relative as my mother had decided not to marry. As a result, the jewellery she wore for her wedding was borrowed except for a gold *arasi* (thumb ring with a mirror) and a gold *challa* (thin ring). My father wore a deep purple, striped sherwani over a kurta pyjama. The few people who came to the reception left by 5 pm. There were no *baratis* (people from the groom's side) except one, Bandu Mehrotra, who came from Indore to represent the Segal family.

Before the wedding they stayed with my mother's sister and brother-in-law at Tagore Town in their cottage. During this time my mother taught their three-year-old daughter Salima some dances and, one day, while she was standing in one of the niches in the drawing room, Ammi was called for lunch and little Salima, who was still in the niche, stayed there till half-way through lunch, waiting for orders to come down!

All the photographs of the wedding, which were taken by Mr Zaidi, were destroyed when his studio was burnt down. Jawaharlal Nehru (Panditji) was to host a wedding dinner for my parents and present them with a pair of Persian carpets, but he was arrested on 12 August 1942 and taken to Poona Jail. When Dr ZA Ahmed, Ammi's brother-in-law who was a prominent Communist leader, went to see him on his release, the first thing Panditji asked was, "How is the young couple?" When Ammi heard this, she said, "You should have asked him, 'Where is the pair of carpets?'

Owing to the disruptive train schedule because of the riots, my parents had to overstay in Allahabad for a week and then in Dehradun for another week, where Memphis had invited them, before returning to the Almora Centre. As there were no quarters for married couples at the Centre, they white-washed and converted a two-roomed coal-shed into a cottage!

My father painted tribal figures on the walls of the cottage, dug up the front portion and made a garden with flower baskets hanging here and there. It became the talk of the town and soon people from Almora were coming down to see it! This teacher-pupil marriage created an awkward situation for them

Kameshwar and Zohra as Shiva and Parvati in the dance ballet

and everyone else around till eventually they decided to leave the Centre in June 1943. At first they stayed with Ranjit Rai (a very old friend of my father's from the Almora Centre) and his parents, adjacent to the Ganga Ice Factory (which they owned) in Lahore. Later, my parents shifted to 32 Empress Road in

Zohra's father-in-law (extreme right), known as Chachaji, was very fond of singing

Lahore, which was very spacious. It was a huge bungalow belonging to the Khannas and my parents stayed in one half of it. Here they started their own institute, which they called the Zoresh Dance Institute, in October 1943. My mother, being more experienced as a dancer and teacher, thought she would be the director of the institute, but my father would have none of it; so they fought and many tears were shed before they decided to become co-directors. They drew up a three-year course and with one stroke of the brush my father designed the cover of the brochure.

They both taught dance separately and Ammi also took classes in several girls' schools and colleges. Professor GD Sondhi of Government College, Lahore, commissioned my father to compose a dance ballet. That was when the troupe performed

Shiva Parvati in Lawrence Gardens, now known as Bagh-e-Jinnah. My mother played Parvati and recalls how she had to jump into Daksha's *yagna* (fire ceremony) as Sati. Later, at her birthday dinner, it was discovered that she had been three months pregnant and that she should never have taken that risk.

Their regular pupils were about six girls, including Indu Chatterjee (now married and settled in Islamabad and teaching dance) and two boys. The late Mohan Khokar, who later studied other forms of Indian classical dance and then became the Secretary of the Sangeet Natak Akademi in Delhi, was one. He was a passionate devotee of Uday Shankar and during his last days in Kolkata he stayed with him and brought out a book on him with valuable photographs. The other boy, Ghanshyam Jayanagarkar, opened a school for dance, Raks-e-Pak, in Karachi, after Partition.

After a couple of years, Shaukat Omar, a friend of my parents, encouraged them to go on tour with their students and offered them fifteen thousand rupees in the form of financial assistance. My parents sat in a locked room to count the money and when that was done they threw it up in the air, not believing their good luck! They toured all across India with their solos, duets and group compositions, among which was an allegorical ballet, *The Serpent*, which showed how the British wormed their way into India, gaining power, but were finally made to leave by the people of this country. Other dances included *Palki, Fisherman's Dance, Burmese Dance, Cowherds Dance, Lotus Dance* and *Katputli Dance*. Timir Barun, who was earlier Dada's music director, was appointed their music director. Ali Akbar, who later became a famous sarod player and Omani

Dasgupta were among some of the musicians who worked with my parents.

Just as they were about to leave on a tour, Timir Barun opted out for reasons unknown to my mother till today and Ali Akbar took over. Horen Ghosh, who had been conducting Dada's tours in India for years, agreed to work for them. Although their tour met with great success, they were penniless at the end of it because Horen said that there were no profits. Many years later, Horen had a horrific death—he was found surgically cut up and stuffed into a suitcase!

MANY MOVES

My parents had started their tours in Lahore going on to Amritsar, Dehradun, Lucknow, Bareilly, Moradabad, Indore, Asansol, Dum Dum and finally in July to Kolkata, dancing at the same New Empire Theatre where my mother had had her first public dance performance on 8 August 1935 with Uday Shankar. From Kolkata they returned to Lahore, disbanded their troupe and went to Mumbai. Here, from 41 Pali Hill they again started their own dance group, known as the Segal Ballet, in the mid-forties. They had regular shows over the weekends at the Sarabhai Hall on Charni Road. A tour with a ballet was

With Uday Shankar, during rehearsals at Elgin Road, Kolkata. First publicity photographs

With Uday Shankar and his mother, Kolkata

due when Mahatma Gandhi's assassination took place and everything was cancelled.

It was at that time that my father got more interested in film direction. There was a group of progressive writers comprising Khwaja Ahmed Abbas, Mulkraj Anand, Kaifi Azmi, Majaaz, Miraji, Mukhdoom, Jan Nisar Akhtar, Kartar Singh Duggal, Faiz

Prithviraj Kapoor and Zohra as Sher Khan and Khairunissa in Pathan, *1947*

Ahmed Faiz, Krishan Chander, Sardar Jafri, Habib Tanvir and Aneel d'Silva. It was the latter who suggested that they should form an All India People's Theatre which came to be known as IPTA, the Indian People's Theatre Association. This was formed in the early forties before India had gained Independence. Balraj Sahni, Chetan and Uma Anand, Bhisham Sahni, Damyanti Sahni (Balraj Sahni's first wife), Amita Malik, Iqbal Malik, Sahir Ludhianavi, Shakeel Badauni, Romesh Thapar and his wife, Dina Pathak and her sister Shanta Gandhi, Hamid and Uzra Butt, Homi Setna, AB Saran, Vishvamitra Adil, Bharat Vyas, Krishan Dhawan, Shahid Lateef, Ismat Chugtai, Krishan Chander, Rajinder Singh Bedi, SD Burman, the famous music director, the folk singer, Prem Dhawan, Salil Chowdhury, another famous music director and several others became its members.

Prithviraj Kapoor was nominated as one of its presidents. Every few years these nominations took place and in 1946 or 1947 my mother held the post of Vice President. Any actor, writer, dancer or painter who had the freedom of India at heart became a member of IPTA. Soon the movement spread and centres were established in all the main cities across India. In Kolkata, Utpal

Zohra maintains that she has always loved to act and that it is her only ambition

Dutt and Shambhu Mitra also became prominent members of this movement. Full length stage plays, street plays, poetry sessions, dance and music performances were held but none of the artists or members demanded a fee. During some of their performances in Mumbai they were harassed by Morarji Desai's party. That was when Ammi wrote to Jawaharlal Nehru who was Vice President of the Interim Government in 1947. Now she says she was cheeky enough to write, "From one Vice President to another!" But sure enough the harassment stopped.

In 1945, PC Joshi, a Communist, formed a group of dancers and musicians known as the Cultural Squad and asked my mother to take charge. She was very excited and decided to go ahead. But, after discussing it with my father, dropped the idea. He pointed out that as she was already employed by

With Romesh Thapar in Waiting for Lefty

Prithvi Theatres, it would be very difficult to do justice to either job. Therefore, Shanti Bardhan was appointed in her place. The cultural squad comprised Prabhat Ganguly, Gul Bardhan, Jitendra Goloi, Abani Dasgupta, Ravi Shankar, Shanta Gandhi, Narendra Sharma, Sachin Shankar and many others. Narendra Sharma had composed a ballet on Jawaharlal Nehru's book *Discovery of India* with which the squad toured successfully all over India.

Initially, Ammi did two Urdu plays with IPTA, *Dhani Bankey* and *Naukrani ki Talash*,which also starred Shaukat Azmi. Later, she became a prominent actress of the English drama section of IPTA. Two important plays that she remembers working in—*They Came to a City* by JB Priestley, directed by Hema Kesarkodi with Uma Anand, Safdar Mir and BK Nehru and *Waiting for Lefty* by Clifford Odets, directed by Mulkraj Anand with Romesh Thapar, who played her husband. Connected with the Bengal famine, Khwaja Ahmed Abbas wrote and directed the film *Dharti ke Lal* (Children of the Earth).

After Independence IPTA lost its impact as its main purpose had been achieved, but nevertheless some of its staunch members kept it going. However, due to IPTA's leanings towards the 'Left', many members decided to opt out later.

Acting as a 'foreign woman', Prithvi Theatres' Deewar, *1958*

EAGLE EYE

Thoughts of my childhood bring back many memories. Ammi could be very strict when needed but, as a child, I could never understand why. When we were in Mumbai and she was employed by Prithvi Theatres as dance-director, she used to take me with her to Opera House in Charni Road—the theatre where the troupe used to rehearse and perform. Opera House still exists. Her 'eagle eye' would be on me all the time. She would make me practice with the theatre boys and girls and, if there were no dances to be rehearsed, I had to sit in the auditorium and not budge an inch while the troupe rehearsed. When there was a reading of any play, I would just sit with the group and listen. I tried sometimes to go and sit in the canteen outside but was soon brought back! We used to commute by bus or train all the way from Pali Hill to Charni Road. First it was a walk to Pali Naka from where it was a bus ride to Bandra station and then the local train. It was a tiring and tedious journey but she did it day in and day out. When the Prithvi Theatres' shows were on I participated as a child artist in quite a few, except for *Ahooti, Paisa* and *Gaddar*. During these shows I had strict instructions to sit in the wings and, being an obedient child, I did just that. I hated *Gaddar* in which my mother played an old *naukrani* (servant) and became older scene by scene.

'Making up' in those days was quite a journey on one's face. First the base, which used to be in a tube and had to be initially applied with little dots and then spread till it became an even layer; then the shading, highlighting, then this thing called 'puff', which attacked you and you lost yourself in a cloud which you thought you could never come out of and, finally, the water spray and patting every part of your face 'into place'! Lipstick, eyebrow pencil and mascara were the icing on the cake.

As the 'foreign woman' in *Deewar* her portrayal used to embarrass me. In the play she wore Western clothes, kept smoking a cigarette and flirting with men. The story was about two brothers who were very close and lived together with their respective wives but are finally separated due to a foreign woman who enters their lives. This leads to their home being broken up by a wall that divides the house into two—reflecting the 'Partition of India'. Even now when she is flirting or being naughty with the opposite sex, I cringe; my brother and I really suffer! Had I not been her daughter, I would have also enjoyed her comments, like everyone else. But, being her daughter, I just can't and very often when she is uttering these embarrassing comments to an interviewer, if I am in the same room, I just walk out.

Ammi joined Prithvi Theatres in October 1945, but she initially started with the theatre as a dance-director. She said that Papaji was so large-hearted that he never said 'no' to anybody who wanted to join—she reflected for a while and added, "Except me!" Apparently he had refused my mother when she initially wanted to join his theatre and so she joined as dance-director. Being with Uday Shankar in her younger days and having worked out his teaching syllabus at the Almora Centre (she was one of the teachers there), Ammi had all the experience needed and this helped her immensely when she joined Prithvi Theatres.

In Prithvi Theatres' Gaddar

She was extremely strict and very good as a teacher. I don't think anybody ever missed her classes at the theatre. My mother never took any nonsense from anyone and knew how to put the 'cheeky ones' in their place. She would start off the class with the body warming exercises which she had learnt under 'Dada' (Uday Shankar) and then proceed with the dances—revision or new compositions. This was also my initial training in dance with her. She had an excellent dancer in a young boy called Suresh Bhatt who went on to give dance-direction for films. She had composed a 'Shiv Tandav' piece for him which he danced exquisitely—I still remember him taking those high leaps and turns when he did the dance. Some of her other disciples were Ruma Ganguly, who was Kishore Kumar's first wife; Gopa Lal; Hira; Indumati Lele, who has her own group of dancers now; Kumud (Lele) Shankar, who married Sachin Shankar; Satyanarayan, who became a dance-director in Bollywood; Prayagraj Sharma, the famous film scriptwriter and several more who have made a name for themselves in one field or another. In any case, all the actors of Prithvi Theatres were students of my mother—even now, whenever Shashi Kapoor meets her, he starts doing all the hand exercises which she had taught him!

For a child it is very difficult to disassociate yourself from the make-believe world of theatre. Theatre and real life all become one. The play *Shakuntala* had my aunt Uzra Butt in the lead role of Shakuntala opposite Prithviraj Kapoor as Dushyant and I was one of the insignificant children running about in the ashram. Since my mother was not in the play she would sit in the wings and watch. In a scene when Shakuntala bade farewell to everything and everyone in the ashram, the atmosphere was one of pain and sadness. Each actor on stage was crying and

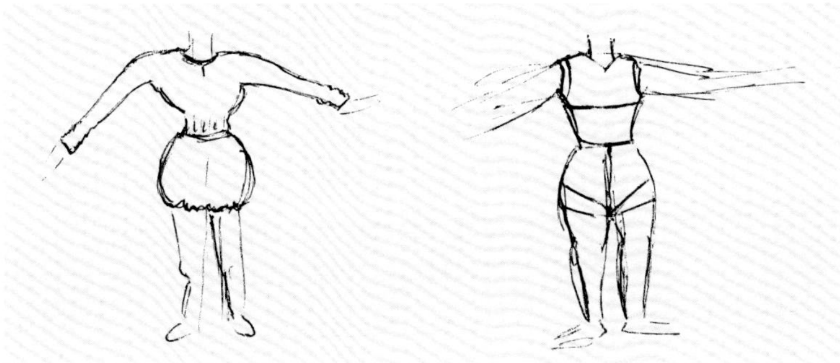

Dance exercises, sketches by Zohra

there was little me actually crying hysterically because I thought that my aunt was really leaving us for good! When Shakuntala was leaving the ashram, everyone would follow her out. I was also in the queue and I remember that even when I reached the wings I could not stop crying.

My mother, who was sitting in a chair in the wings, put her arms around me and asked, "*Tum ro kyun rahi ho* Kiran?" (Why are you crying?) To this I replied that I thought my aunt would never come back. Ammi hugged me—I can never forget that warm reassuring hug—and said, don't be silly, this is only a play. My aunt, who had noticed me crying immediately said, "*Dekho main to yehin hoon. Main to kahin nahi ja rahi. Yeh* theatre *hai*, theatre!" (Look, I am not going anywhere, this is just theatre!) It was a very strange feeling, like everything going out of focus. But it was indeed difficult for me as a kid to draw a line between reality and make-believe.

Ammi is also my very first Guru in dance! As a kid I enjoyed dancing but what I did not enjoy was the strict discipline it demanded. Even when I was about eleven or twelve years old, I remember my mother choreographing dances on me when all I wanted to do was to go out and play with my friends. Whenever I was free from school, she would take me to Prithvi Theatres with her and there, apart from being under her

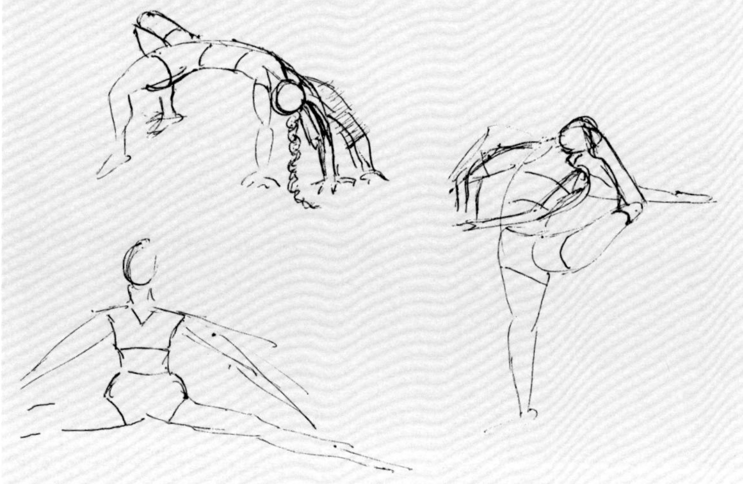

Dance exercises, sketches by Zohra

'eagle eye', I also participated in all the warming-up exercises and dances with the other theatre artists. She was very, very strict as a teacher! From the Uday Shankar style I went on to Bharatnatyam and finally Odissi. In my teaching it is my mother's training that has helped me a lot. Quite unconsciously I have absorbed her discipline and patience. Over the years I have also created several body exercises, which my disciples learnt and are using in their teaching.

When asked by Sheila Dhar what she enjoyed most in her varied career ('Meeting Zohra Segal', an interview that took place almost twenty years ago), Ammi said, "Teaching. I'd have been a great teacher, I know. Far better than I was a dancer or actress. I realised this when I was a dance-director at Prithvi Theatres. As an actress I have earned much money, prestige, even the love of people. But, I had the advantage of sharing the limelight of others—first Uday Shankar, then Prithviraj. But because of my looks or for some other reason, I lacked star quality. If I had been able to have a school or performing troupe of my own, where I could have taught, I would have been a great person. I am sure of that."

Ammi had composed dances to Rabindranath Thakur's poetry with music by Salil Choudhury. I still remember a couple of tunes. I was supposed to give a solo dance (my very first) to a poem *'Baul baul, bajaye, bajaye, bajayere, bajayere ek tara...'* Rehearsals were very enjoyable and great fun, but on the day of the show I got stage fright and, when my turn came, I refused to move. My mother, who was standing behind me, felt me clutching her and saying, "*Maine nahin jana*" (I do not want to go), to which she ordered, "*Kaise nahin jana*" (How can you not go) and gave me a solid push (or so I thought)! Once on stage, I enjoyed myself thoroughly and have been doing so till today.

Another incident comes to mind that took place in Porbandar, Gujarat, around 1953. Pavan was just a baby and he was also on tour with my mother and me as part of the Prithvi Theatres troupe. We were all sitting in Prithviraj Kapoor's room one morning and his faithful servant Pyarelal (a boney man with lovely shiny brown skin, huge moustache, *banyan* [vest] and khaki shorts) brought in Papaji's chai and placed the tray on his bed where Pavan was crawling. Everyone was too busy talking and no one noticed Pavan aim for the teapot! Within seconds the boiling tea was on him and he shrieked and shrieked! Huge blisters appeared on his right thigh and leg—the doctor arrived immediately and my mother held on to her baby boy who was howling with pain while the doctor cut open the blisters. I distinctly remember how he cried and with every shriek my heart shrieked as well. Had I been the mother, I would have broken down, but Ammi just held on to him firmly. She held back her pain and tears for the sake of her little son. I sometimes wonder if so much holding back and control is good.

Kiran as a little girl, photographed by her father

PALI HILL

Mumbai's 41 Pali Hill was where we all stayed. By 'we' I mean Chetan Anand, Dev Anand, Vijay Anand and their sister Savitri Kohli, whom we kids called 'Maati'. She was with her six children and her two other sisters. To us they were Usha Aunty and Bonnie Aunty and of course Uma Aunty who was Chetan Uncle's wife and their two kids 'Kunki' (Ketan) and 'Gunnu' (Vivek), who was always roaming about *nangu-pangu* (naked). Since this house was built on a hill it had odd entrances. If you approached it from atop the hill the Anands' level was the ground floor and our floors were beneath, but if you entered the house from our entrance then the Anands' floor was the second floor! The landlords, Mr and Mrs Cork, with their sons Allan and Noel and Mrs Cork's dogs who always followed her like bridesmaids, lived right on top. Mr Cork was fair, had brown hair and tiny blue eyes. He was a thin man. Mrs Cork also had fair skin, golden hair (coloured or not, I couldn't say), light eyes, which at times seemed green and sometimes grey, depending on where you were standing and how drunk she was; there was always a cigarette hanging from her lips and from it ash hung on 'for dear life'. The Corks were perpetually having a drunken brawl (at least that is what we kids thought), regardless of what time of day it was. Ammi and Dost, although very happy, had separate bedrooms for reasons unknown to me. She informs me now that he used to snore very loudly!

Mumbai was just becoming a famous melting pot for artists in film, theatre and dance. Chetan Anand was in the process of establishing himself as a director and so was the young Vijay Anand; Dev Anand was an aspiring young actor. He had already acted in a few films under the Navketan banner. Guru Dutt, who was also a friend of my parents and, therefore, a frequent visitor, was making *Baazi*, starring Dev Anand and Geeta Bali. Ammi had been asked to provide the dance-direction for *Baazi*. I remember being taken for the shooting of a song-and-dance sequence by Geeta Bali and a group. The song was *'Dek ke akeli, mohe barkha sataye re, galon ko choomein kabhi chintein udaye re, tip, tip, tip, tiptiptip.'* All the dancers had polka-dotted umbrellas, which they used for a particular dance movement. In those days shooting was extremely uncomfortable—there was no air-conditioning; huge fans would be switched on between shots and switched off during the shooting. There would be pin-drop silence once the shout of 'SILENCE' was heard. The make-up man would be perpetually on duty with his 'pancake', 'puff' and 'mirror'.

Navketan produced a film called *Nau do Gyarah* directed by Vijay Anand, in which Ammi was asked to do the dance-direction. This was Waheeda Rehman's first film in which she played a vamp. I was on the sets of the film and could not understand why they had made her wear a horrible pink dress but, of course, it came out fine in the black-and-white film. The other films that Ammi provided the dance-direction for were *Badnam* starring Balraj Sahni and Shyama, directed by DD Keshav, and Helen's first film, *Faraar*, starring Kishore Kumar. Ammi also acted in this film.

In Pali Hill I have memories of my parents always laughing and joking! My *chachas* (father's brothers)—Leelam Chacha

Kiran with her father

(Leelanath Segal and his wife Kunjbala Chachi) and Nannu Chacha (Triloknath Segal and his wife Madhuri Chachi) used to come and stay with us from time to time. It was like a 'happening', that's what it was! So much would be going on.

A major period of great excitement and celebration in our house was the festival of Deepavali. Dost would make beautiful lamps that looked like cylindrical Chinese lanterns and place them on the stairs of the house with a candle inside them. The paper these lamps were made of was greased and, therefore, became transparent. He would paint beautiful designs on them and when the candle was lit they would look so very festive. We would have the fireworks in the garden and that was the finale of the evening!

Everyone from 41 Pali Hill would come down to our place to witness the fireworks. My father would organise everything so beautifully. There would be the *phirki*s on one side and every child would get a *phooljhadi* (sparkler) to hold, *anar*s (another kind of sparkler) were a special attraction and, finally, the small red *patakha*s (crackers) lit in a *balti* (aluminium bucket) or a *mutka* (empty terracotta water vessel) of which the top would be closed so that the lit *patakha*s made such a racket that it was quite unbearable and yet enjoyable. Little black pills, which turned into twisted snakes when lit with a matchstick, fascinate me even today.

Incidentally, or fortunately, both my *chacha*s married outside their community. Leelam Chacha married a Gujarati and Nannu Chacha, a Nepalese. My father, a Hindu, married a Muslim. I say fortunately, because due to all these mixed marriages, I have not grown up with any kind of hatred towards any caste or creed; nor did my parents ever teach me to prefer one to the other.

Ammi and I would sleep on a large hard bed covered with white sheets and a huge *machchardani* (mosquito net). She always insisted that I should sleep in the afternoons, which I

Fussing over her son Pavan's turban; photograph by Kameshwar Segal

hated. These days I would give anything to find time to sleep in the afternoons! Ammi was and is very particular about the bed sheets, pillow cases, bedcover and towels being changed once a week. I remember our sheets were always snow-white. *Anjeer* (figs) were hung on the outside of the mosquito net for us to eat early in the morning. "Good for the stomach," my parents would say.

When the *dhobi* (washerman) came, she would meticulously take the *hisab* (accounts) while I jumped all over the dirty clothes, much to the *dhobi*'s and my mother's annoyance. Ammi tells me that she didn't know housekeeping and learnt it only after marriage. She is very proud of the fact that she always had servants to do the work. In order to get her interested in housework, my father organised a *dhobi* book for her and drew miniature clothes in the margins.

I remember the Goan cook, Lewis, giving her the daily account of the amount spent on groceries and so on. He wore khaki shorts and a short-sleeved vest that never seemed to be quite white. My mother wrote down whatever he recited every evening regarding the daily purchases. Then their totals had to be tallied, followed by a minor tiff if they didn't. He would always ask about the next day's menu and I remember my favourite words such as 'puteen' for pudding and 'cutless' for cutlets and 'phish phry' for fried fish! Lewis was a thin, frail man, but very sweet. He would make lovely 'baingan ka bharta' in which he gave the 'lassan ka bhagaar' on a burning coal. It was delicious! There were no mixies then, and all the masala was ground on the *silbuta*. I used to love watching Lewis grinding the masala—it was like magic. My mother was not very happy about my going into the kitchen and chatting with the servants. She would always say, "*Bete, naukaron mein mat baitha karo! Yeh achchee aadat nahin hai*!" (Do not sit with the servants. This is not a good habit!)

Although she didn't know any cooking and other housekeeping chores, she was unbelievably neat with sewing, using a thimble on her middle finger while stitching. Once, sitting near our

With her sisters-in-law and their families, Madhya Pradesh

bedroom window in Pali Hill, she was stitching something that was orange and it had a sheen to it. The moment I rushed into the room, she hid it behind her back, much to my annoyance. My curiosity would not let go. I kept insisting that she should show it to me but my pleas fell on deaf ears. Noticing that she was smiling all this time, I had an inkling that the hidden treasure was meant for me. Later, when I saw it on my birthday, I was amazed by the beauty of the orange colour and all the *zari* and *gota* (gold embroidery) on my *gharara* (skirt) and kurta. I still can't forget that orange!

Birthdays for me were great fun. Ammi and Dost always invited a lot of people. My birthdays were never a quiet affair—loads of people, loads of presents and my friends and I running all over the house. The thing I enjoyed most about my birthdays was tearing open the presents or, actually, the wrapping on the presents.

My childhood background was very 'Indian'—in the sense that we never wore any artificial material, only cotton. My parents and their friends never wore any Western clothes unless they were Anglo Indians or Indian Christians. We generally spoke in our mother tongue, although the medium of instruction in my school was English. My parents and relatives had seen India through the 'freedom struggle' to gain her independence. They looked up to Gandhiji, Jawaharlal Nehru, Sarojini Naidu, Dr Rajendra Prasad and all the others who led India to her freedom. My cousin had to stay with us as a child because her Communist parents had to go 'underground' during the freedom struggle. Except for my school uniform (cotton), all my clothes were 'ghagra choli', 'salwar kameez','churidar kurta' or 'garara kurta'. We never wore Western clothes, apart from my father who sometimes wore trousers and a bush shirt when he went out. I clearly remember my father in pyjama kurta (in those days the pyjamas were really wide) and my mother in cotton saris.

The irony is that, despite all this, I was sent to a convent school—St. Joseph's Convent. Most of my friends from school wore dresses, frocks, skirts and blouses (they also wore Indian clothes) and these fascinated me, till one day I decided to have a dress for my birthday. Ammi would always ask me before my birthday what I would like to have as a present and this time I said a 'dress'! She was so disappointed, she tried her best to talk me out of this choice. She even tried to use my aunt Uzra to persuade me to change my mind, but I was stuck on that one 'dress' which had to be white with a light blue creeper going across it. The tailor was called, the dress was stitched—in taffeta—and I wore it on my birthday! Here, I must mention that

With her brother-in-law Triloknath Segal and his wife, Madhuri, in Madhya Pradesh

although my mother disapproved of certain things in my life, she has never stopped me from doing them.

My father used to paint in Pali Hill, his canvases were used in Chetan Anand's *Neecha Nagar* in which he also gave the art direction. When I saw the film recently, I enjoyed it thoroughly although it was dismissed as a flop in its time. Now it is considered a 'classic' in Indian cinema. Both my parents acted in it, but my mother had a longer role, which I thought she did very well. My father was seen here and there in groups, smoking a cigar!

When we moved to Carter Road, I don't remember him painting. He used to get work in bits and pieces but the regular breadwinner was my mother whose employment at Prithvi Theatres kept the house running. She has always worked very hard all her life. Once my father earned quite a lot of money and as a present for my mother he got a Godrej refrigerator, which was kept in the dining room in one corner in Pali Hill. This was the same dining room where a cobra had slid in during breakfast. My mother was on my right at the table and my father on the other side. John, the 'boy', was bringing the breakfast and the 'breadwallah' had come for his payment. He had entered the dining area and was standing near my father. There was a jungle on one side of our house and the cobra came in through one of the windows. On seeing it, my mother shouted, "*Hai meri bachee*!" (Oh, my child!) and I stood up on my chair. Her arms were outstretched towards me. My father said, "*Koye nahin hilega*!" (No one is to move!) We were all frozen on the spot, but the poor 'breadwallah' around whose feet the cobra was promenading was trembling and perspiring profusely! The cobra reigned this moment, he was king! There was a silence full of fear in the room and then the cobra went around my father's chair, almost like doing a *parikrama* (circumambulation). It literally stood on its tail, looking like one long, black rope. The cobra then shot out of the window—an unforgettable picture that is stamped in my memory.

During this period I was studying in St. Joseph's Convent in Bandra. My parents never pressurised me with my studies, they were just happy that I did not fail. They were more happy with the fact that I was the captain of my house, 'Tennyson' and was extremely good at country dancing (it was a convent school!) and at sports.

Once Ammi was on tour with the theatre. Since I did not have any holidays, I could not accompany her. So there I was in Pali Hill with my father, my paan-chewing ayah Itaabai, Lewis and

At a picnic with her in-laws—Zohra in an emotional moment with her brother-in-law Leelanath Segal

John to take care of me. I had a thick growth of hair, very similar to a horse's tail! It was very difficult to take care of and I would not let anybody touch it except my mother. She had and still has very soft hands. For the entire period that Ammi was on tour my hair was in a mess and when she returned she was shocked at what she saw. Being such a tidy person herself and so particular about hygiene, she just could not believe her eyes! The surprising thing was that she never said a word to me; she just made me understand that I should never let this happen again. She sat patiently and spent hours brushing, combing and literally unknotting each strand of hair so that I could look 'normal' again.

On another tour with Prithvi Theatres we were performing in Belgaum and I got lice in my hair. Ammi was so horrified and shocked that during the day she would take me for a long walk in an area that was covered in red sand or bricks and sit quietly, taking the lice eggs out of my hair! There was no 'Lysol' and 'Medicare' in those days. Incidentally she also played 'Snookums' (a cartoon character) with me—just to keep me amused! Guess who was 'Snookums'...not me!

Mr and Mrs Cork, the landlords of 41 Pali Hill, Bandra, decided to migrate to Australia with their two boys Allan and Noel and Mrs Cork's battalion of dogs. I don't know if the dogs made it to Australia, but the Corks definitely did. So, 41 Pali Hill, where I had spent some of the happiest moments of my childhood, was sold. The new owner was interested in constructing a high-rise building. I was in Mumbai recently and went to see what 41 Pali Hill had become. It was shocking. An ugly piece of architecture had replaced that beautiful house and only a part of our garden still remained. Since we were of no use to the landlord monetarily, he decided to get rid of us and ordered/asked/requested the individual families to go and find accommodation elsewhere in Mumbai. The Anand brothers (Chetan Uncle, Dev Uncle and Goldie Uncle) moved to Juhu with their respective families; Savitri Kohli stayed on with her children in 41 Pali Hill to move out to Juhu a few years later; my parents, Pavan and I moved on to a small flat in Perry Road and then to a larger flat on Carter Road, near the sea.

My childhood friends, Munni and Baba (Aruna—now Mrs Parikshit Sahni and her brother Yash Kohli) got left behind in 41 Pali Hill. They were on top of the hill and I was near the Arabian Sea! Yet we visited each other quite often. One afternoon, when I was at home with just the cook and ayah, I was paid a surprise visit by Munni and Baba. Delighted at meeting me, they coaxed me to join them to go and see a Hindi film at Bandra Talkies, which was near Bandra railway station. Initially I refused, saying that I would have to take permission from my mother who had still not returned from the theatre. They kept persuading me and I kept refusing, saying that Ammi would be very angry if I did something without asking her—even Dost was out for the day. Munni and Baba would have none of my excuses and after what seemed like an eternity I ended up being persuaded to go with them. As we got off the BEST bus and crossed the road, who did I see standing in the bus queue—my mother! *Mera to khoon sookh gaya* (my blood just dried up). I was caught 'red-handed'. She saw me and shouted, *"Kahan ja rahi ho? Chalo ghar mere saath"* (Where are you going? Come home with me). Saying this, she dragged me in line with her. I stood behind her in the bus queue. My feeble excuses fell on deaf ears. Munni and Baba were stunned, I was in a state of shock. I wanted to be in the cinema hall rather than go home with my mother, but she kept a firm grip on me.

Within seconds the bus arrived and systematically everyone started boarding it. As my mother got on, the conductor stopped me from boarding the bus. Something inside me said "goodie" but Ammi said to the conductor, *"Arey ye to meri bachchi hai"* (She is my child) and then he made a gesture allowing me to board the bus. I pretended as though I didn't understand him and stood firmly on the ground, watching my 'angry mother' being taken home by BEST.

Munni, Baba and I bought our tickets (they treated me) and we saw the film (I forget which one it was). We felt very independent and grown up and thought we'd return home *'seena taan ke'* (triumphant)! Coming home was a different story altogether. Once inside the gate, I started trembling with fear and before my mother could spot me I rushed to the bedroom and hid under a quilt. Then the dreaded moment arrived. My mother found me, she pulled up a chair right next to the bed where I was bundled up under my 'quilt-fort' and shouted, and shouted and SHOUTED! Was she annoyed, upset, furious. (These are mild words.) I still remember some of the sentences she used: "You'll be ruined if you don't listen to your elders. You'll run amuck if you don't obey your parents"...God knows what else. Of course under that quilt, I kept wondering what 'amuck' meant! With every shout, I thought now she's going to hit me, now I'll get one. Luckily that never happened. Ammi has never hit me till today.

Our Carter Road home in Bandra had two bedrooms and bathrooms, a tiny dining area, one kitchen and a garage. My parents gave it on rent to Manasa Ram, an actor from Prithvi Theatres. Its servants' quarter was right near the sea. One just had to walk across the road to step into the sea. I went to Mumbai recently and visited Carter Road just for 'old times' sake'. I was horrified to see no more sea in front of my old home's gate. Instead, there was a row of cars parked there, then the 'Joggers' Park'—one had to search for the waters of the Arabian Sea! This house was used for the filming of *Dil Chahta Hai*.

FACING DEATH

I think my parents had had a tiff the previous day and in the evening Ammi and I had gone to see a play. When we came back my father's room was shut and we kept knocking but there was no reply. He would very often lock himself up in his room for days and practice tantra, so we were used to it. But this time the knocking went on for a long time! I was a skinny kid so my mother asked me to slide my hand inside the slightly ajar bathroom window and open the bathroom door. I did as I was told and went inside to see what had happened. To my surprise I saw my father lying on his stomach on his bed fast asleep—or so I thought! Soon my mother followed and knew what had happened—he had taken an overdose of sleeping pills.

I had never faced death and did not understand anything except that I had lost something very close to me, very early in my life.

As the formidable Lady Lili Chatterjee in UK-based television series Jewel in the Crown, *1982*

I felt empty and suspended and was very disturbed by all the crying and cries that filled our home for the next few days. My mother showed immense control over her emotions but every now and then she would suddenly break down like a mad woman and shed uncontrollable tears. I have never witnessed her crying like that ever again. I would just stand quietly behind doors and watch silently, as though stunned. Even now, as I am writing this, I cannot hold back my tears. Papaji and the entire Prithvi Theatres came to console Ammi, but of course nothing would help. In fact, Papaji's presence was a great support for my mother who had to go to the police station with Papaji to give a statement—a note had been left by my father or else my mother could have been implicated. At one point I remember my aunt Uzra looking at me standing behind a door and remarking, "*Isey deko, isey tho kuch hua hi nahi hai; ek ansoo nahin hai iski ankh mein*!" (Look at her, nothing has happened to her; she has not even shed a tear!)

After that fateful day—12 May 1959—everything changed in our lives. My younger brother was still tiny and eight days later was his birthday. He kept asking, "Dost *kab aayenge?*" (When will Dost arrive?) and my mother had to hold back her tears and just pretend as though he was about to turn up. Both of us (Pavan and I) were sent off with a cousin of my mother's (Dr Hamida Saiduzzaffar, Director, Gandhi Eye Hospital, Aligarh) who looked after us for a few years. Meanwhile she packed up everything in Mumbai and came to Delhi.

Ammi had resigned from Prithvi Theatres in 1959. She then wrote to Panditji and Kamaladevi Chattopadhyaya, asking for a job. When she arrived in Delhi she stayed with an old friend,

Ranjit Rai, 'Bapu', as we kids used to call him and his lovely wife Kamala or 'Amma' to us. They were friends of my parents in Lahore before Partition. Ranjit Rai had even come to Almora to learn dance. They had and still have a beautiful bungalow at 3 Prithviraj Road. Sadly, Bapu is no more but, being with Amma is like being with him all over again. She has one of the most beautiful smiles that I have ever seen.

Kamaladevi offered my mother the post of principal of the Delhi Natya Academy for Dance and Drama under the Delhi Natya Sangh in October–November 1959. She then went to

Zohra conducting dance classes at Begum Zaidi's Hindustani Theatre in Delhi, 1960s. Kiran is behind her (first row, left, in white sari)

Mumbai for a month to take a sort of crash course in teaching drama from the renowned theatre director Ebrahim Alkazi. She also attended Herbert Marshall's (Director, Bombay Natya Sangh) classes in acting when in Mumbai. Ammi thinks she stayed with Uzra who was then living with her husband in Soona Mahal in Marine Drive, Churchgate. Referring to all the 'Rabindra Bhavans' built in India by the Government, Herbert Marshall would often observe, "This is like putting the cart before the horse, since there isn't any theatre activity to show in the theatres!" On her return to Delhi, she stayed with her elder sister and brother-in-law in 136 North Avenue. Both were staunch Communists and he was a member of the Lok Sabha, which is why they were living in North Avenue.

The Delhi Natya Academy opened on 3 February 1960. Joy Michael of Yatrik fame was the Vice Principal, Sushma Seth (nee Mathur), the famous film actress, was the movement teacher and the late Pandit Amarnath, the renowned vocalist, was the music teacher. I remember our classes being held at 34 Shankar Market. Yamini Krishnamurthy, a young and beautiful dancer, came to Shankar Market with her father to give us a lecture-demonstration on Kuchipudi and/or Bharatnatyam. Ammi also went to various colleges such as Miranda House, Hindu College and Indraprastha College to teach dance. At that time Krishen Khanna's father was the Principal of Delhi Public School, Mathura Road. He invited Ammi to take dance classes in the school. Begum Zaidi, who was the President of the Delhi Natya Sangh and owner of the Hindustani Theatre in Delhi, requested Ammi to give movement classes to the theatre actors. Habib Tanvir was a leading director as well as the founder of this theatre.

Joy Michael, Vice Principal, Delhi Natya Academy

Taking 'movement classes' in Delhi

I would accompany Ammi to most of her classes and would even perform her choreography; take, for instance, the poem, '*I carried my curds to the Mathura fair....*' by Sarojini Naidu. Ammi would very often use poems and interpret them into dance. There was one called *The Bird Catcher* which Jeffery Phillips 'Kama Dev' and I used to perform in England for my mother's lecture-demonstrations. It always used to go down very well with the audiences.

With her children, Kiran and Pavan, in Hampstead, London, 1965.

Photograph by Prithviraj Kapoor

LONDON LIFE

Three years after my father's death my mother left for England. She arrived in London on 18 April 1962 to do a ten-week refresher course at the British Drama League in Fitzroy Square. She remembers that Mr Elmhirst of Dartington Hall had deposited one hundred pounds in her name at the National Westminster Bank in Fitzroy Square. There were students from almost all the Commonwealth countries, some older, others younger than her. Kunwar Sinha (a well-known documentary filmmaker in Mumbai) was also doing the course with her. Ammi says she has never enjoyed herself so much as she did in those ten weeks. She shed all her inhibitions and became like an eighteen-year-old! She lived in a students' hostel for the duration of the course.

With documentary filmmaker Kunwar Sinha, Trafalgar Square, 1962

Left to right: Kiran's friend, Jean Steer; Dr Hamida Saiduzzafar; Zohra's younger brother, Ikram; Zohra and Pavan, London

Ammi had arrived in London via the USSR where she had been on a lecture tour on Indian dance and theatre. During this period China attacked India. Ammi was panic-stricken and she promptly sent for my younger brother Pavan and me. Passports, visas and so on were taken care of—it was not difficult since my uncle, Dr ZA Ahmed, was an MLA in the Lucknow Assembly. Without much hesitation we were packed off on an Air-India flight to London with Pavan vomiting most of the way. It must have been terrible for him.

Arriving in London was a shock! It wasn't like what we had seen in the films in India. Now, due to television there is so much more exposure about what is going on in the world around us. At that time, one got a view of the West only through films, American and British—mostly American. London was dreary, dull, dark and all the shades of grey that one could think of. I was so unhappy! As it is I was miserable at having to leave all my friends in college (Lady Shri Ram) and then setting foot on this grey canvas. Ammi had taken on rent a tiny flat on the top floor in Abingdon Road, High Street, Kensington. It had two bedrooms, one teeny-weeny kitchen and an even teenier-weenier bathroom in the attic that was perpetually frozen. I

Zohra, Kiran and Pavan with Prithviraj Kapoor, London, 1960s

shudder when I think of it now. We had no servants and all the housework had to be done by us. Even the shopping, house cleaning and cooking! My mother could not cook then. Her cooking at that time was by trial and error; she had no choice since she now had the responsibility of feeding her two children. One day she decided to make chapattis and I saw her struggling in the kitchen. Not being able to bear her suffering any longer, I offered to help and finally made the chapattis myself. It was one of the most wonderful things that could

Left to right: Alice Bonner, Uday Shankar, Beatrice, Uzra and Zohra, Dartmoor, Devon

have happened to her, and she remarked, "I never knew you could make chapattis! Why did you keep it a secret?" To this I replied, "Well, if I'd told you, you would've roped me into making chapattis every time." Gradually she became one of the finest 'self-taught' cooks that I have known, except that she puts too much oil.

In London we would always have people over for lunch or dinner and every time she would bring these sumptuous meals to the dinner table. She also became an expert 'paratha *wali*' (maker of parathas). She could line up a lunch or dinner for at least ten to fifteen people single-handed. Now, Ammi doesn't cook and dislikes the food that is generally cooked in the house, saying that it is 'wishey washey' and boring. But when she is on her own (if I am on tour) then she makes 'yum yum khana' or else she will order it from outside! She loves chillies–the more the merrier. Despite doctor's orders to eat less chillies, she says, "What does he know; it is good for my digestion. I must clear my system." Strange isn't it— yet green chillies seem to be her best friends. If the green chillies are feeling lonely, then red ones are added as well— just to keep them company! But, ever since our return from Kerala in April 2005, she is taking 'dal mein tadka' in coconut oil and her system is fine. She insists that it is the coconut oil! Maybe she is right.

However, to come back to our life in Abingdon Road, things were quite tough since we had to do everything ourselves. Our

At Bryan House, Hampstead, London, 1937

Top: With Kiran, Prithviraj Marwah, Pavan and Kunwar Sinha, London. Photograph by Prithviraj Kapoor.

Below: With Pavan and Ikram, 1967

landlady was an Indian Christian called Mrs Roach who had a very beautiful daughter who had also worked as my uncle's (Mamu's) secretary. We had no television then. Mrs Roach had a black-and-white set and she would sit in front of it the whole day, huddled up in a quilt with the paraffin heater next to her and a kettle of hot water on top of it, which was perpetually boiling. I have no idea what she did with that water, whether she made tea from it or used it in a hot water bottle or just enjoyed the hissing sound of the steam. Pavan had started enjoying television viewing and would slide, literally slide, his little body through the slightly ajar door into Mrs Roach's drawing room and with her permission sit 'glued' to the television! Mrs Roach would sometimes wear a knitted cap if it was too cold; there were strands of grey, wavy hair peeping out from beneath; she was dark in complexion and possessed big, round eyes, which one felt had X-ray vision!

Straight from India, we were not used to all the hard work but Ammi helped us in understanding the system. She would show us how to shop, count the currency and, of course, say her favourite word—thank you—every time. A particular brand of butter that was available was called 'Anchor Butter' and we would giggle every time she would ask for it across the counter. It was the way in which she would pronounce it, making it sound like 'Ankaw'—very British indeed! We didn't know what a 'laundromat' was and, when Ammi took us to one, it was such fun to see all those clothes going round and round, washed, rinsed, spun and dried! Later it was very boring! I had a difficult time trying to understand the 'cockney accent' of the Londoner. Nobody in London speaks English the way we are taught in school in India.

During rehearsals, UK

This was a very, very difficult period in my mother's life. Without a regular job in theatre or films or television, she now had the responsibility of bringing up two children. Pavan was put into school and I joined evening classes in sketching and drawing at the St. Martin's School of Art on Tottenham Court Road. I would commute by the underground train (tube), wearing a duffle coat, jeans and polo neck sweater, carrying a portfolio full of sketches. I used to feel terrible underground and whenever it was overcrowded and the tube stopped for a while I would feel uncomfortable. I even fainted once. When I came to my senses it was surprising to see so many worried faces around me, asking "Are you all right deary?", "Do you feel better now?", "Aw, you poor thing!"

In order to make both ends meet, Ammi was doing two jobs. During the day she would work in a store and in the evenings she would work as a 'dresser' in the theatre known as the Old Vic. She never looked tired and always had a very happy face.

With Ben Kingsley during the filming of Harem

As Mrs Bhandari with Dierdre Costello in Our Own People*, 1981*

Once, when I accompanied her to the Old Vic, I was horrified to see my mother just helping these actresses dress. It was bad enough seeing her like this, but what made it worse was seeing these actresses running about in their 'birthday suits' without batting an eyelid! To them it didn't matter who came into the room, male or female! You can imagine my condition—raw from India, still a little shy, being exposed to so much. My mother saw me feeling uncomfortable but never said a word and 'braved her job like a soldier'. Also, she was used to this nudity, which she had experienced in her earlier days in Dresden where she had gone to study 'dance pedagogics' (teaching dance to children). She told me that when all the dance students would change she would hide behind her coat and change, unlike the other girls. This must have amused the girls but, knowing that she was from India, they would have understood. The Old Vic was near Waterloo station, pretty far from where we stayed but my mother braved it through all the seasons with amazing courage and grace. To watch the play *Peer Gynt* starring Leo McKern, I was seated in a box very close to the stage and I definitely felt very special but could not understand a thing about the play! I also saw *Othello* during its dress rehearsal at the Old Vic. It was easier to understand.

Some years later we shifted to a lovely spacious flat in Lyndhurst Gardens in Belsize Park, very near Hampstead. The flat was huge with three large rooms and one small room with a bay window. There was a kitchen and a fairly big bathroom. It was on the first floor and the area we lived in was very green. I had a lovely room all to myself with a very large bay window that overlooked the curving road beneath. I was then completing a diploma in Display and Design. My room was always untidy; it was the 'in thing' to be that way. This used to irk my mother who herself was and is an extremely tidy person (a bit too much)! Even at this age she has a special place for all her things and remembers in which plastic bag they are. She has this habit of wrapping up everything in small plastic bags, one inside the other—even a tiny safety pin will be in some remote place in a drawer, which will have to be 'dug out' as per her instructions. It's very irritating when you are in a great hurry and need the safety pin immediately!

With Dolly Ahluwalia (extreme left) and others during the shooting of the television serial, Amma and Family

Ammi would often get irritated by the way my clothes used to be lying about, my portfolio, brushes, pencils, colours, records and so on. Her biggest threat was, "You are not going out on Sunday, until and unless you clean your room." Much against my wishes, I would put away my clothes, hoover my room and put everything back in its place. This really annoyed me but now when I look back, it's such a laugh!

One evening, when my mother and I were coming home, we witnessed what was known as 'Paki bashing'! It was a terrible experience seeing a group of skinhead boys beat up a man, kick and rob him and run away and nobody could do anything. In fact, there was nobody around except my mother and I, who were on the other side of the road frozen, shocked and horrified. This was the first time that I had seen violence in real life. We did not know whether this man was Indian, Pakistani, Sri Lankan or Bangladeshi, but he was from this subcontinent. The poor man slowly stood up, collected his stuff that was strewn all over the pavement and went on his way.

Actually this kind of hatred was rising due to the sudden influx of Bangladeshis, Punjabis and also East Indians. A lot of this immigration was also illegal. I think this was the time of Enoch Powell who politically was inciting a lot of hatred against Asians among the British.

Ammi decided to send Pavan to a boarding school near Ipswich. Every time he came home for his holidays it was lovely and the saddest thing was his going back. I used to hide my tears but my mother was very strong and would always bid him a smiling goodbye, despite the sadness on his face.

A scene from Amma and Family, *directed by Vaseem Dehlvi; the series became a huge hit*

We were staying in Viewside Lodge, Highgate, when Walter Botschi, my fiancé, came to ask for my hand from my mother. I had no idea when he would arrive, so I got busy setting one of my wigs on her head. It was dripping wet, for the curlers had to be put into it. Just then the doorbell rang and Walter walked in! He was horrified to see Ammi in this way and just could not control his laughter. Ammi was equally embarrassed and burst out laughing but still allowed him to marry me! She was and still is very fond of him and was very unhappy when we separated and then finally divorced in 1980.

In Delhi, 1987, after her return from England, my mother did a television series *Mullah Nasruddin* (directed by Amal Allana), which initially gave her a lot of publicity. She then acted in another series, *Amma and Family*, directed by Vaseem Dehlvi, which was a great hit with the common man. There was one

Delivering another wonderful performance in Amma and Family

episode where she did a double role. Her original character was that of a grandmother and her double was an actress from England, very westernised and very 'full of herself'. I thought Ammi gave one of her best performances in that role. I often teased her after that and told her, "I am sure this is what you really wanted to be!" Of course, she just laughs it off.

Many years later, on 29 May 2004, I received a letter from my mother who was busy shooting for *Chicken Tikka Masala* in Preston, UK. This is with reference to the 'red-green chilly world'. She wrote: "The weather here is absolutely lovely. For lunch we have very good vegetarian and non-vegetarian food from a 'Gujjoo' restaurant...for dinner I order by room service, some of the dishes are not bad. I usually spice up the stodgy soup with extra hot chilly sauce and add green chillies to the cole slaw-mayonnaise garnish, which they serve with every sandwich order. The garlic bread is also nice, but I am already looking forward to home-cooked food and home sweet home!"

THE ENSEMBLE

Ammi was in England and had been there since March 1962. I was in Delhi in 1973 to brush up on my Bharatnatyam when Ammi decided to come to Delhi for a short while. During this time Maya Rao, the famous Kathak dancer and choreographer, now living in Bengaluru, was taking classes at 34 Shankar Market, where Ammi was earlier running the Delhi Natya Academy. She invited Ammi to give a talk to her students. Initially Ammi refused, saying that she was no good at giving speeches but could talk informally to the girls and boys. However, when she started to speak at 5 pm the talk went on till 10 pm. Ammi spoke of her life and her experiences as a dancer and stage actress.

Usha Bhagat, Social Secretary to Indira Gandhi and Shanta Gandhi, Director, Bal Bhavan, were also present. When it was all over, they were very excited and said, "Zohraji, now you should come back to India!" To this Ammi replied, "Unless I have a decent job, I cannot leave England." So, Usha Bhagat spoke to Indiraji whose idea it was to start the National Folk Dance Ensemble in Delhi, where a group of dancers would be trained to perform folk dances of the various states of India. It was opened with the Prime Minister's funds for a one-year pilot scheme. Ammi was called from England to take charge as director. Her diploma in pedagogics in 1933 from Dresden, Germany, her experience in forming the five-year dance syllabus for the Uday Shankar Dance Centre in Almora in 1940, her fourteen years' experience as a dance-director in Prithvi Theatres, as principal of the Delhi Natya Academy and as the

Taking 'movement classes'—Usha Bhagat (facing Zohra) is on the right

principal of the Ram Gopal Dance School in London, all helped in setting up the Ensemble curriculum.

Although the emphasis was on folk dance, Ammi had asked Sharmaji (Narendra Sharma) to take classes in the Uday Shankar style of training. The dancers would be given intensive and rigorous training in the folk dance styles and would perform, when required, in front of visiting international dignitaries. Though their training was thorough and their first stage show on 11 March 1975 in Mavalankar Hall (due to Kapilaji's help and encouragement) a great success, the idea did not take off because of strong opposition from the Sangeet Natak Akademi in Delhi. The pilot year did not get completed. Their excuse was, that they did not want to undertake the extra responsibility of running the budget of the Ensemble as "they were already overburdened with work".

The Akademi even suggested to Indiraji that the Ensemble should be made into an autonomous body but nothing came of it. Indiraji was much too busy attending court sessions in Allahabad so in a huff she gave orders to close the Ensemble. The artists' world of Delhi was shocked and a committee was formed—Save The Ensemble Committee. Meetings were held at which prominent artists such as Ebrahim Alkazi, Indrani Rehman and several others expressed their views against the closure. While the director, my mother, was away, the students of the Ensemble did an Oraon folk dance in the Rabindra Bhavan lawns, protesting with placards. This caused a sensation and Indiraji was compelled to rescind her earlier decision and give another three months for the continuation and re-fashioning of the Ensemble. Seventy Members of Parliament signed a petition saying that this has to continue and Dr ZA Ahmed was persuaded to head the delegation to Indiraji. The next day Emergency was declared! Of course anything to do with the artists' world fell into the background. My mother had worked her heart and soul to get this off the ground and when it did not happen, she was heartbroken; she packed her bags and went back to England, only to return in 1987.

In England, she was offered a twenty-six episode series called *Padosi* (Neighbours) by the Further Education Department of the BBC with the role of coordinator for each episode. This involved introducing each episode and also acting in it. Her co-actors were Roshan Seth, Indira Joshi, Soni Razdan, all of whom are big names now. The programme was shown three times a week and the entire series was repeated. She played the role of Mrs Choudhry. This was when Ammi became a household name with the Asian community.

Always a strong woman, Zohra showed remarkable courage when she battled with cancer in 1994

HIGH SPIRITS

Ammi has unbelievable inner strength. The year 1994 was a bad one for her—a lump in her right calf turned out to be a tumour and she had to undergo surgery. She put up a very brave front all through the tests, examinations and biopsies. I would hear her screaming from pain and there was nothing I could do standing outside except feel the same pain. Pavan told me that if the tumour touched the bone then she would be bed-ridden for life—I was devastated and just could not hide my feelings. Pavan was stronger than me; I was to leave for a performance, which I was going to cancel but he insisted that I carry on with my dance tour, or else she would know that something was seriously wrong with her. But she knew. She tells me now, "The moment I saw the expression on your face, I could tell that I was seriously ill."

I was performing in Udaipur; waiting for my call to start the performance, I have never prayed to God as I prayed that night and asked Him to save my mother's life. However, it was just her strength and only her strength that made us see her through the illness. At Ram Manohar Lohia hospital she was under the able supervision of Dr AK Banerjee who was then chief of surgery. I was so relieved to have such a wonderful doctor take care of her. For, not only was he such a good doctor, he was also very caring and humane in all his dealings with his patient. My two disciples, Anuradha and Sudha, stayed at the hospital with Ammi, while I shunted back and forth between home and hospital, cooking and bringing whatever she felt like eating. She hated the hospital food! Pavan stayed in the hospital with her for a couple of nights as I had a pain in my back. Satyanarayan, my vocalist/friend, was also of great help in this period and so was another friend of mine—Bela Singh.

Dr Banerjee was so taken up by my mother that one day he brought his entire family to meet her in hospital and till today we have all remained friends. Here I must mention SPIC MACAY. It was owing to my meeting Mukulika, Dr Banerjee's second daughter, that all this treatment and surgery was possible. (She was the SPIC MACAY representative on one of my lecture-demonstration tours—I think it was in Madhya Pradesh.)

My mother was full of laughter, jokes and funny comments. At times she would tease the young doctors and the nurses who took some time in seeing the funny side of the comments. All this went on throughout the day and I sometimes wondered what my mother's last thoughts were before she fell asleep.

When she was discharged and brought home, she still had to go to Batra hospital for Radiology sittings. I think it was almost every day or every other day. Seeing all the other cancer patients was very painful but even there she kept her spirits high and was full of fun. All along her illness, I felt it was she who was giving strength to us rather than the other way around. She had almost lost sensation in the right leg and yet she walked for one hour every day with a zeal that was quite unbelievable! I am sure she's got a 'self-charging' battery inside her.

VIGNETTES

1980s onwards: Lunch has to be served at 12.15 pm. I think living with me has elasticised Ammi a bit and she doesn't mind if lunch is half-an-hour earlier or later. She is very particular about her 'figure', like a sixteen-year-old starlet. She weighs herself almost every week and if she goes a little bit above then, at lunch, it is one toast instead of two and in proportion every other intake is diminished. Although she is fussy about her diet, Ammi does not mind it if, once in a while, there is no soup or if she has to have a regular lunch instead of the usual soup and salad. This used to happen sometimes when I had no regular help at home and had to rush off in the mornings for a lecture-demonstration or a meeting. I often make fun of her and then she has a go at me: "Look at you. You're just letting yourself go.

A poignant moment in Din ke Andherey, *directed by Ebrahim Alkazi, Delhi, 1990s*

According to Kiran, Zohra has always been very particular about her 'figure', like a sixteen-year-old starlet

As a dancer you should be more careful—you are just getting so fat!" She is right and it has made me get back to my routine of daily walks, rehearsal and exercises. But when I feel like teasing her I call her, 'Fatty'!

In the evening, when she has finished her walk, she sits down to read or work on the *Times* crossword. It is an addiction with her. When my aunt Uzra was with us, the two of them would attack the crossword, which they did successfully and came out victorious! From lunch onwards, she does not eat anything and is naturally famished by 9 pm, which, incidentally, is dinner time. Dinner is our main meal, if it gets delayed for some reason then I have to hear, "*Aaj kya baat hai, khana nahin khana* [What's up, don't you want to eat dinner]. I am so hungry. Kiran, don't you realise that I haven't eaten anything since lunch!" To this I reply, "Then have something now." Then there is an adamant "No". Earlier I would have dinner with her, now, if I am not hungry, I just don't eat.

The funny thing is that when we have people over for dinner then pangs of hunger don't disturb her. She enjoys a couple of drinks with them and has a great time with all the 'attention'. Incidentally, Ammi can knock back her drink just like a taxi driver. But then, it's just a couple and no more, after which she starts exclaiming, "I'm sure I'm drunk"—of course she isn't. Ammi just loves an audience and gets very bored if nobody takes any notice of her. Once in Delhi we had been invited to a reception. The evening was very enjoyable, meeting lots of friends one had lost touch with. When we returned home, I exclaimed, "Oh, what a lovely evening it was!" To which she immediately replied, "*Kya* lovely evening—*mera to kisi ne* notice

POWER

hi nahi liya!" (What lovely evening—no one took any notice of me!) I just burst out laughing, it was too funny.

Ammi is just like a little child at times. You've got to see her when guests are at home and she has dressed herself in a new outfit. We have a duplex flat (her room is on the top floor). She actually comes down the stairs as though she is making an entry on stage and laps up all the praise when her presence, outfit and so on are admired with 'oohs' and 'aahs'! (This was a few years ago, now it is difficult for her to even take a few steps without someone's help.) Not one for being shy, she can easily talk to anyone if she wants to and also snub anyone if she is not interested—something which I can never do!

Discipline, stubbornness and starch go hand-in-hand with my mother. Her entire day is worked out to the minutest detail. Up at 7.30 am, three or four glasses of water to be drunk, followed by breakfast at 8 or 8.30 am, comprising just one mug of hot coffee and nothing else. Then she will go back to her room to literally scan the daily newspaper, have a bath, do some paperwork and then get down to her daily routine of exercises, which she does for nearly an hour-and-a-half. Exercising is the most important part of her routine. If, for some reason, she misses exercising in the morning, she makes it a point to find time later during the day. Once she was climbing the stairs and I was watching her very intently, she noticed this and, as if she could read my thoughts, said, "Do you know the secret of my health—it is activity my dear, activity."

Facing page:
Another delightful performance in Amma and Family, *Sanawar*

Ammi is as stubborn as a bull. Once she decides on something, she just will not budge—whether it is good or bad. She loves starched clothes, I hate them. My daughter loves them. As a kid I remember Ammi's saris would always be starched and worn 'properly' to the last pleat. I hardly remember her wearing silk in those days. I think her character was reflected through the way she wore her sari—neat and firm—hand bag under the armpit, never slung and, of course, an umbrella was a must. Her hair was always neatly plaited and then tied into a *jooda* (bun), a hairstyle which has not changed in all these years. Come to think of it, I have never seen her with her hair open except when she has washed it or when she is doing a particular role in theatre which demands it. Ammi's hair is silver now; even as a child I remember a few strands of white. For that she blames my father, who she says was perpetually trying out hair concoctions on her. She wore a 'kumkum' bindi (there were no 'stick on' bindis in those days), tiny gold earrings in the shape of a *kairi* (mango-shaped) and two thin gold bangles and her wedding ring, which is now with me. After Dost's death she refused to wear any jewellery except in her plays, or television or film roles. She looks very nice with a little jewellery but she refuses to wear any; I have tried very hard to persuade her, but it is all in vain.

24 May 2004: I had just come back from PVR Cinema in Saket, New Delhi, after seeing Mani Ratnam's *Yuva*. It was brilliant!! Actually, very nervously and excitedly, I'd gone to see my daughter Sujata who was acting in the film as Ajay Devgn's sister. Sujata was wonderful and very natural. Had my mother been with me she would have been thrilled to bits. Sujata has appeared in several serials—*Kaisa Ye Pyar Hai, Dhoom Machalo Dhoom, Yehan Ke Hum Sikander, Love Ne Miladi Jodi* and, more recently, *Devi*. All of us, especially my mother, watch her serials

Kiran and her daughter Sujata during a television shoot for Inner London Education Authorities, London, 1973

every Monday, Tuesday, Wednesday and Thursday religiously; Ammi being the most serious of us all. Sujata has surprised us by her acting skills. Ammi is extremely fond of Sujata and has a very, very soft corner for her, but when the two of them fight, they fight like cats and dogs. A friend of ours once witnessed these fights and remarked, "Gosh Kiran, they fight like sisters."

With, from left to right, Madhyama, Kiran and Sujata, 2009

No sooner is the fight/argument over, they are the best of friends; you'd never believe that a few moments ago they were at each other's throats! It's a strange relationship. I could never dare talk to my mother the way Sujata does. But, at times, I have lost my temper and spoken to Ammi very firmly. It must be painful for a parent to hear one's child shouting at you. But I also get taken to that limit when I say to myself, 'That's it and no more; I am not going to take this any longer!'

22 April 2005: I had accompanied Ammi to Kerala where she was shooting for *Mistress of Spices,* directed by Paul Berges, starring Aishwarya Rai in the lead. We stayed at the beach resort and she did most of her shooting in the nearby surroundings and by the seashore. Since we were sharing the room I was watching her as she walked around unpacking and arranging her things. She was quite unsteady on her feet. I began to worry and wonder how she would go through the shooting. But when she faced the camera she was a different person altogether, bursting with energy and life! One day she filmed from morning till approximately 8 pm. I am sure if the director had not stopped she would have still gone on despite her tiredness, the humidity and the army of mosquitoes. Those were four glorious and fun-filled days that I spent with my mother despite her tiring schedule.

When we got back to Delhi I was surprised and also very touched to hear her say, "Kiran, I am so happy that you came with me on this trip, you don't know what a difference it makes to me." I told her, "Well I hardly did anything except jumping up to answer the telephone and order the food and, besides, you always have someone with you." She replied, "No, no,

As the 'Mad Rani' in Ek Tha Rusty

it's different with you." I was quite flattered. Incidentally, she did the same thing of working from morning till evening when she was shooting an advertisement with the cricketer Shoaib Akhtar. Work started in the morning and didn't finish till the evening. The result was that she fell ill. I have tried to make her understand, but once she is working she loses all sense of time—come to think of it, we are all like that!

23 May 2005: I had just returned from Fab India with a beautiful two-seater *mondhah* and another single *mondhah* to replace the awful three-seater that we have at home. Now, Ammi does not like all this, and the moment she saw it she started running it down, saying, "Only people who cannot afford wooden furniture buy this kind of furniture; it becomes dirty very soon and it pokes the arms" and any other excuse to run it down. I cannot understand how she can dislike such a lovely craft. She remarked, "They are just meant for being in the verandah."

BIRTHDAYS

Ammi is a great one for 'thank you's' and 'please's'! She gets very upset if you don't thank her and sometimes I don't—just to annoy her. Also, her 'good mornings' and 'good nights' are equally important. It was her birthday on 27 April 2005 and I took her out to dinner. We could not do much as we had just returned from Kerala; I didn't even have time to buy her a birthday present. However, at dinner I saw that she wasn't looking quite happy and I thought that it was just the tiredness of the journey. But, to my surprise, it wasn't that—the reason for her unhappiness was that there was no birthday cake! So I quickly went and ordered one and told her that it had all been worked out and organised beforehand, which was a lie.

Enjoying ice-cream with Preity Zinta and Divya Dutta in Veer-Zaara

With Dolly Thakore, announcing the 'Ladli of the Century' award

Actually I thought that she must or should have 'grown out' of birthday cakes and all that; but to my surprise she was very pleased and said, "Now I feel it's my birthday." Such a kid! Amita Malik came and met her at the table and so did Krishen Khanna and his wife Renu and some other friends. She kept telling all of them that it was her birthday and that she had completed ninety-three years!

Once, when she was eighty-nine, I gave her a surprise birthday party. She had absolutely no idea of what was in store. I had invited all her friends and asked each one of them to cook something and bring it along. The day started very normally with me wishing her and then, later in the morning, I said to her, "Aren't you going to get ready and put on some better clothes?" She didn't seem to think it was necessary but I forced her and so she changed. She was looking rather unhappy and neglected! At 1 pm her friend Alfred Wuerfel turned up to wish her, she was quite taken aback. Then Usha Bhagat came, followed by Amita Malik, Pavan and his wife Seema and their kids Rohan, Taamra and Anoushka. Soon it was Joy Michael and then Rati Bartholomew and several others who could make it—each one with a lovely dish. Some of my friends also dotted the invitation list and generally we were all having a grand time. Then her birthday cake, which had a huge eighty-nine written on it, was brought into the room by Pavan. You should have seen the delighted expression on her face, she was just like a five-year-old. I wish I had taken a photograph!

Now, every sixth month, she makes some excuse to replenish her wardrobe with new clothes and off she goes shopping with me if I have the time or with a friend or disciple of mine. I enjoy going with her because then I can make her buy me a salwar kameez or a beautiful sari. Even now I manage to get some money out of her around Dussehra saying, "Where is my pooja sari and what about my birthday present?" In her youth I have never seen her wear salwar kameez except in plays when her role demanded it. She was always in a sari and a salwar kameez was like a night suit for her. These days she hardly wears a sari, it is salwar kameez all the time; she says that now it is more convenient and practical for her.

When she is busy she hates going as 'chief guest' to any function but when she is a little free she doesn't mind at all. In 2005, she had been attending almost every other function where she has been invited as chief guest or she was being honoured. Ammi thinks she is a *kunjoos* but actually she is 'pennywise and

pound foolish'; for example, once she went to receive her sister from the airport and for assistance she took Suresh, our house help, with her. She made him wait in the taxi instead of taking him inside to help with the luggage and the trolley because she did not want to spend another fifty rupees on his ticket. Also, I can get money out of her at the drop of a hat—it is another matter that I never do it, except for my pooja sari, Deepavali sari and my birthday present!

Above and facing page: Enjoying festive moments with Salman Khan, Aishwarya Rai and others in Hum Dil De Chuke Sanam, *directed by Sanjay Leela Bhansali, 1999*

I have tried my best to persuade her to open up a 'Birthday Greeting' agency. Sounds crazy doesn't it? Ammi is a great 'birthday card sender/greeter'. If she gets to know your date of birth you will religiously receive a birthday greeting card from her, year after year. What's worse is that she insists that I should also sign the card. Earlier I would just refuse to sign and she would go on and on and finally I would succumb! Now I just sign as a reflex action, at times I do not even know to whom she is sending the card. Oh yes, every letter, every day, is very important and has to be posted immediately. Despite my explaining to her that the letterbox has been cleared for the day and will only be cleared by 10 am the next day, so the important letter can be posted the next morning, she insists that it be put in the letterbox immediately—as if by some miracle her letter will be taken by a fairy called 'the postman'.

One thing I really admired about Ammi was that, until recently, her New Year cards to her friends all over the world were personally sketched and drawn by her. Her colours would be red, dark blue or dark green combined with some pen and ink. She would begin this beautiful exercise somewhere mid-October and carry on till November. All her friends and relatives would receive her handmade cards in time for Christmas and the New Year and also reply. During this period her room acquires a very happy look with the cards displayed on her table and bookshelves. In fact, not just her room but the whole house gets a very festive look. Actually, the festive look starts from Deepavali and carries on till well after New Year.

LOVE OF POETRY

As a little child Ammi hated poetry. She says this is due to the fact that one of her friends, Mumtaz Shahnavaz, also known as 'Taazi', would always try to hold her and cuddle her, which she hated! Mumtaz Shahnavaz wrote beautiful poetry!

Much later, in Mumbai, when she was with Prithvi Theatres, Prithviraj Kapoor asked all the artists to memorise and recite a poem by Hafeez Jalandhari, *Nagma-e-Bahar* (The Song of Spring), which he used to recite beautifully! On 8 December 1983, Raviji (Pandit Ravi Shankar) was organising a festival at Delhi's Siri Fort, in memory of his elder brother Uday Shankar.

At a poetry recitation event; Zohra has a great variety of poems in her repertoire

He asked my mother to contribute something for this occasion, which she did in the form of a recitation of *Nagma-e-Bahar*—*'Abhi to main jawan hoon...'* When she appeared on stage she announced, "This poem is an offering to my two Gurus—the gestures to Uday Shankar and my voice to Prithviraj Kapoor!" She brought the house down with her recitation.

In 1989, when Safdar Hashmi was brutally murdered, there was a gathering at the Sangeet Natak Akademi in Delhi in his memory. His family asked her to recite poetry. Her lack of a repertoire in poetry and her lack of knowledge of Urdu poetry led Safdar Hashmi's family to give her a poem to recite by Faiz Ahmed Faiz. It took her three days to memorise and five minutes to recite this very powerful poem called *Intesaab* (Dedication). During these three days she realised how the poet has dedicated it to the pain and suffering of people in every walk of life.

Over the years, Ammi was in great demand for her poetry recitations and so she added a variety of poems to her repertoire. Now she has poems for children, poems about Partition and speeches from her plays, some in English some in Urdu, in her repertoire; she has been invited to open several festivals, functions and important gatherings with her recitations.

I recollect, it was around 1995, when we had been invited by a very dear friend who was in the Indian Army to have a holiday in the mountains. On several occasions he and his wife had invited us to spend some time with them. Shamelessly, we had always accepted and enjoyed our holidays, courtesy General Mohanty and his beautiful and courageous wife Bharati! Once we were in Kausani, having a gloriously peaceful holiday. One day the colonel in-charge wanted Ammi and me to spend some time with the Army officers and their wives. During cocktails he requested Ammi to give her recitation of the famous poem, '*Abhi to main javan hoon*'. She doesn't sing it like Malika Pukhraj used to, but recites it, giving every verse her own interpretation as she understands it. The most important piece for the listener is the last line of every verse, *Abhi to main javan hoon*. Each time she says it, she has a different tone and expression in her voice.

Well, this evening it wasn't meant to be, because although the 'Army audience' sat enraptured by her—every time she came to the last line the colonel would 'pop in' with arms swaying here and there and, like a kathak dancer at the end of a dance *tukra* (piece), he would put his arm out and orate loudly, *Abhi to main javaan hoon*. I was noticing how Ammi's mercury was rising after every verse and when she finally finished, she turned to me and uttered, "Idiot—ruined my entire poem!" I was in fits of laughter but had to put on a serious and sympathetic expression (being a dancer helps!).

With Jamila Verghese in The Caucasian Chalk Circle, *Delhi, 1962*

FLASHBACKS

Ammi once observed that it is unusual that, in spite of Rampur being an insignificant estate, it has made a name for itself because of the Nawab's intelligent and innovative brain. Nawab Hamid Ali Khan grafted mangoes and created a species known as 'samar bahisht', which means fruit of heaven. Baba (Ustad Alauddin Khan) had told her that the Nawab's knowledge of music and dance had elevated the name of Rampur in the artistic world. He popularised the *Char Baith*, which is the poetry sung by Pathans. Ustad also said that the standard of the *domni*s (girls who danced and sang, they are not prostitutes but can be kept as mistresses) was elevated to a professional and classical status in the world of music and dance. The Nawab had several known musicians and dancers in his court, including his court dancer Kalka Bindadeen. We children were also told that the Nawab had crossbred a 'pointer' species with a street mongrel and started a new pedigree known as the Rampur Hounds. These hounds proved to be excellent retrievers in hunting. Ammi recalls how my father would call out, "Here come the Rampur Hounds" when her relatives would visit her!

The other day she was talking about Rampur and remembered how Baba—who had run away from his home in Bengal as a boy—began his career. When the Nawab of Rampur's carriage was approaching, eleven-year-old Alauddin Khan threw himself in front of it. The Nawab asked him what he wanted, the little boy begged to be allowed to study music under Ustad Wazir Khan, who was the lead musician of the orchestra at the

Rampur court. Having an orchestra was a rare innovation in India at that time, that is, in the early twentieth century. She also remembers, on one of her trips to Rampur, at a function, peeping through the *purdah chik* and seeing the venerable white-bearded, old musician, Ustad Wazir Khan, conducting the orchestra with a pencil-thin ivory stick. She was awestruck and went back to Queen Mary's College and told all her school friends about it, since in those days there were no such things as orchestras. Ammi recollects Baba telling her that when Ustad Wazir Khan accepted him as his disciple he was taught nothing for two years and only allowed to fill his hookah and press his feet. This was the old *guru-shishya parampara* (master-student tradition). Baba studied the sarod under him and later became the foremost sarod player of India.

When television had just been introduced in India, Ammi did two plays for Doordarshan—*Diya Bujh Gaya* directed by Shivendra Sinha (I think it was the first play for television) and *Saat Paise*, directed by Habib Tanvir. Along with this she did a lot of stage plays such as *The Caucasian Chalk Circle*, directed by Inderlal Das, founder and owner of the Little Theatre Group (LTG); *Shatranj ke Mohrey*, directed by Habib Tanvir; *The Waltz of the Toreador*, *The Heiress* and *The Lark*, directed by Tom Noonan of the USIS. This was in the early 1960s.

Another memory I have is of the time when Ammi came to Delhi. She wrote for *Shankar's Weekly* as the drama critic. One evening she was going to review a performance and was keen that I should go with her. I do not know what happened to me, but I just got it into my head that I did not want to go. I was in my teens then—sixteen or seventeen. She kept insisting and I kept refusing! Finally, much against my wishes, I had to accompany her, grumbling all the way and muttering, "I don't want to go with you!" Ammi then turned around and angrily told me to go back home. It was dark and we were walking from North Avenue to the Secretariat bus stop behind Rashtrapati Bhavan. I turned around to go home and I had barely walked a few steps, sobbing, when a man held my arm and asked me why I was crying! That did it, I was so terrified that I shouted "Ammi" and ran to her, and was I thankful that she was still there. She just held my hand and walked with me.

I also remember when Pavan was about to be born, my mother and I went to Nainital. He was born on 20 May 1952 at Ramsey Hospital. We were staying at the Metropole Hotel. In those days it was a lovely hotel and very grand, too. After my father's death Ammi kept taking me to Nainital for the summer holidays. It was also a good time to visit Pavan who was then in Sherwood School. Nana would rent rooms or a cottage so that the whole family could spend some days there. Nainital was very peaceful and quiet then; no cars were allowed after the bus stop and we would go up on horses or *dandis*. The Boat Club fascinated us kids. Since some of us were under eighteen, we were not allowed entry into the Club. On some evenings when we would walk by we could hear sweet music and all the young men and women dancing and romancing to Frank Sinatra, Bing Crosby, Nat King Cole and Louis Armstrong's music.

With Amitabh Bachchan in Cheeni Kum*, directed by R Balki, 2007*

VOICES

In an interview with Sheila Dhar (1992), my mother had explained, "The creative process in my field is different. In both theatre and cinema, you have to be aware of something outside yourself. On stage, it is the audience and on film it is the camera. In theatre you have to throw your voice to the gods. In cinema, you don't have to act at all. The camera close-up catches whatever is passing in your mind or heart. The viewer should be able to see and feel the same thing. To cultivate this skill requires tremendous discipline, hard work,

While acting, Zohra says she is totally consumed by the effort to become the other person and remain in control of herself at the same time

concentration and *riaz* or practice, like any art. But mastering such skills is only the beginning. After this stage, a mad person that lives inside every actor emerges and takes over. I say 'mad' because the actor's personality splits. He is himself as well as the character he is playing and both must be real. The feeling of both halves of the schizophrenic personality must be genuine. If I am weeping, I must tear out my heart and show it to my audience. If I do this artificially it can never move them...I want to be truthful and I have to say that God is not even remotely in my mind when I am acting. I am totally consumed by the effort to become the other person and to remain in control of myself at the same time. One always tries to achieve perfection but that happens very rarely...It is very important to be aware of the significance of the role one is playing in relation to the entire work..."

According to Amal Allana (review of *Stages*), "As a theatre person, this is my reading of Zohra's story. Her's is one of telling of her eventful life with characteristic humour and wit and totally eschewing self-pity. Despite having abandoned the purdah, her personal resentments and disappointments, preferring to maintain at all times her dignity and integrity, surely a fall-out of her aristocratic upbringing. Her book ends with a question she poses to herself, 'Could I have done more?' My answer to that would be, she has done more than enough, and this book, over which she has laboured for over thirty years, comes as a solid contribution to the history of contemporary Indian theatre and dance. Salut Zohra!"

Facing page: In a documentary on Zohra by Anwar Jamal, shot at her cousin Sahibzada Yusuf Khan's house, Rosaville, Rampur

Writes Alfred Wuerfel in *India My Karma*: "While in Bombay until 1953, I met Zohra quite often. I never missed the shows

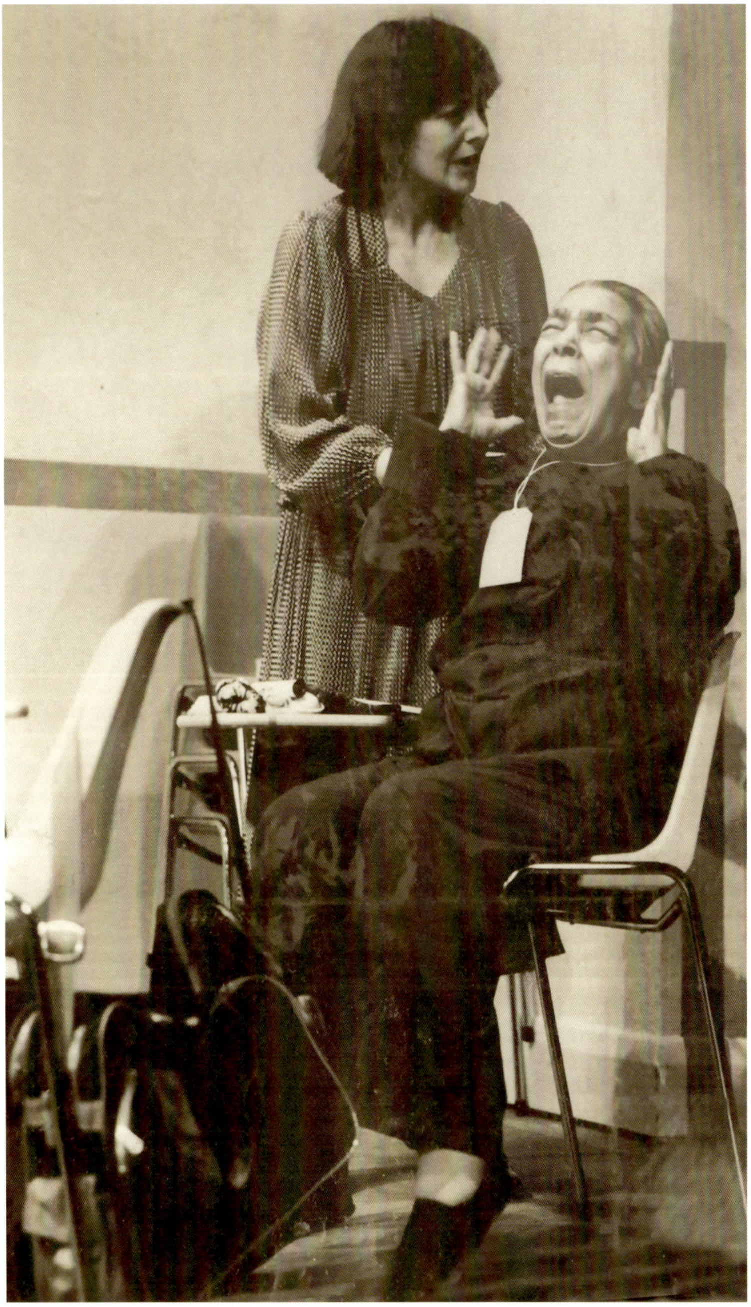

As Mrs Pong in the play,
The Primary English Class

'I want to be truthful and I have to say that God is not even remotely in my mind when I am acting'— Zohra Segal

in which she played the leading roles...In 1950, I was asked to join the German Consulate-General in Bombay and finally in 1953 I was transferred to the German Embassy at New Delhi as a member of its Cultural Department. However, I meet Zohra every now and then and more often after she had moved from Bombay to Delhi. Whenever she meets me, she embraces me and remarks: 'Here comes my oldest boyfriend.' She has become a very successful actress and even now, ninety years old, she still acts in films and on stage and her performances bring the house down...Knowing each other for such a long time from 1930 onwards till now we meet in our homes in Delhi and whenever she appears on stage I am sitting in the front row!"

Cheeni Kum: *Many expressions, many emotions*

THOUGHTS

I was telling Ammi recently that, despite being an adult, I feel like a little kid inside and at times want to do mad things. "That's very good! You should always keep that feeling within you," she said.

I miss putting my head in my mother's lap; I am sure that she must be missing it too. Come to think of it, I just don't have the time. This reminds me of a day when I think I was six or seven years old. My father, mother and I were in my father's room and there was some subject the two of them were going on about! Dost was smoking (his favourite cigarettes used to be Capstan or Gold Flake, kept in a tin which had a built-in cutter that used to fascinate me). I was intrigued by the fact that he used to put a cigarette to his lips and smoke would come out! It

According to Zohra, 'The camera close-up catches whatever is passing in your mind or heart.' With Preity Zinta in Veer-Zaara

was magic! Being very persistent (I still am), I wanted to try that magic. My father kept saying, "No", "This is not meant for little children", "It's not good for you", "You'll fall ill" and so on.

Poor man, he tried his best to dissuade me, but I would have none of it and finally he put the 'magic' to my lips and told me to take a deep breath in and then blow out. Ammi immediately said in an irritated voice, "*Kya kar rahe ho* Kameshwar?" (What are you doing, Kameshwar?) For me at that moment Dost was important. Not realising that he was trying to teach me a lesson, I did as I was told. Coughing and spluttering in a cloud of smoke, dizzy and breathless—I nearly fainted. I did not know where I was going till my mother caught me and put my head in her lap and began to caringly rub my back. In this semi-conscious daze I heard her telling my father, "*Tum bhi kamal karte ho* Kameshwar. *Ek choti bachi ke saath koi aise karta hai*?" (Does one do like this to a small child?) She was very upset with him. But I must say it was one of the most horrifying experiences of my 'little life'. I also remember how very comforting it was when my head was in my mother's lap, as though nothing could harm me now.

Ammi has two very bad habits—one is blowing her nose at the dining table and the second one is when she does not let you even sit down and take a breather when you come home. She starts straightaway with whatever has to be done, or any message that has to be given! Every time she gets the news of someone passing away she exclaims, "*Ab main hi ek reh gaye hoon!* Next will be my turn!"(Now I am the only who is left! It will be me next!) Ammi is happy with all the awards, titles and honours that have been bestowed on her, but ask her where

Across generations—with Swini Khara in Cheeni Kum *(Amitabh Bachchan behind)*

they all are and she will tell you that they are safely packed inside a box with a bedpan! Just the other day she suddenly burst out, "When I die I don't want all of you crying...and be sure to flush my ashes down the toilet!"

Playing the challenging role of the mother of a confirmed bachelor who falls in love with a girl thirty years younger than him, Cheeni Kum

AMITABH BACHCHAN

April 17th 2006

My dear and lovable Zohraji,

As promised on the sets of "Cheeni Kum", I am sending you Champagne. I do hope you enjoy it.

It has been wonderful working with you and your unflinching energy is a great inspiration to all us youngsters.

Wish you good health, joy and happiness.

With very warm regards

Amitabh Bachchan

Ms Zohra Sehgal
New Delhi

amb:rs.jalsa

PRATIKSHA JUHU MUMBAI 400 049

Zohra Segal, dancer, actress, story-teller, lover—lover of all things—and loved by all, notes Tom Alter

ZINDABAD!

I think I first met Zohraji about four hundred and seventy-six years ago, in the Mughal Court, where she was entertaining the Badshaah with her wit and beauty and dancing skills—if the Badshaah was *salaamat* before he met her, he was *sahi salaamat* after doing so...

Then I met her in the former Mughal Court of Dilli in the year of our Lord, 2007—actually, the year was Zohra's, but she let the Lord have his way. We performed William Dalrymple's *City of Djinns* for sixteen magical evenings in a row—or rather, Zohraji performed, and we admired. Blessed those evenings were and she turned a young ninety-five during the run, or the scamper, as it was.

She took less time than Sachin to get to her century—and with a higher strike-rate—no nervous nineties, she was as full of life and love and a touch of lust as she was at the original Mughal Court. And yet, a thorough professional; when people made a fuss about her, she let them know in no uncertain terms that she was just fine and needed no special attention. But she got it anyway—because she is special—and not just because she is making a hundred but because she is Zohra Segal, dancer, actress, story-teller, lover—lover of all things—and loved by all things, great and small and those in-between—including me—and Badshah Salaamat—and thousands and thousands of others around the world.

Zohraji, Zindabad, *aur janam din bahut, bahut mubaarak ho*!

Tom Alter

With Tabu in Cheeni Kum

ACKNOWLEDGMENTS

Many, many thanks to Madhyama, my granddaughter, who patiently helped me with the selection of the photographs. I am also grateful to my disciple Anuradha Verma who sat for hours with my mother, Madhyama and me, numbering each selected picture. And I cannot forget Sujata, my daughter, who provided us with all the entertainment during these hours. Last, but not the least, hats off to my mother, who, despite her age, sat with me recounting moments, events and 'happenings' in her life! Without her this pictorial book would not have been possible!

Bikash and Tultul Niyogi have gone totally against time and have done an amazing job at bringing this book out to coincide with my mother's hundredth birthday! Thank you both!

Also, thanks to Dolly Thakore who, at the last minute, helped me with pictures of some of my mother's Bollywood movies. The *Veer-Zaara* images are courtesy Yash Raj Films Pvt. Ltd.

Kiran Segal